AF575374

THE FOUNDATIONS OF WISDOM

VOLUME 1

LOGIC

THE FOUNDATIONS OF WISDOM

VOLUME 1
LOGIC

FR. SEBASTIAN WALSHE, O. PRAEM.

TAN Books
Gastonia, North Carolina

Cover design by Andrew Schmalen

Library of Congress Control Number: 2022939034

ISBN: 978-1-5051-2636-5
Kindle ISBN: 978-1-5051-2899-4
ePUB ISBN: 978-1-5051-2900-7

Published in the United States by

TAN Books
PO Box 269
Gastonia, NC 28053

www.TANBooks.com

CONTENTS

CHAPTER 1

The Beginnings of Philosophy

The world in which we live is full of things both wonderful and mysterious. Anyone who lives in constant contact with children is continually aware of the wonder which they experience each time they encounter a new reality, or even when they come to understand a new word. I believe it was G. K. Chesterton who observed that, for children, the whole world is new and fantastic; it is just as remarkable to a child that a river should flow with water as with wine since, from his perspective, there is no reason why rivers should have water more than wine. And so, for these neophytes to the world, everything is full of marvels. It is this wonder which is the starting point of philosophy—a wonder begotten of ignorance coupled with a desire to know the reasons for things unknown.[1]

According to the earliest historians of philosophy, the branches of knowledge which were developed first were concerned with practical ends, such as agriculture, hunting, and building. It is natural to suppose that so long as man was struggling to meet the practical needs of his day-to-day existence, earning his bread by the sweat of his brow, there would be very little time to devote

[1] This wonder is not mere curiosity, which is a vice. Curiosity means desiring to know something not because it is good for us to know it but rather because of some unreasonable motive.

to more speculative or theoretical pursuits. But once the practical arts had been developed in such a way that certain men were freed from the bonds of labor and given time for leisure, some of these men began to devote themselves to an investigation of the causes of reality. This investigation was not for the sake of some practical end, but it was pursued for its own sake—that is, for the sake of truth—since there is in man a natural desire to know the causes and principles of the things he experiences.

From the earliest historical accounts of the rise of philosophy, it appears that the first attempts at explaining the world in terms of its causes were poetic in nature. Great theological poets, such as Homer and Hesiod, interwove accounts of the origins of man and the universe within their stories. While these accounts were generally mythological in character, they were notable since they aimed at providing reasons for experiences common to all men: the experiences of nature, human love, war and famine, and so on. And while the accounts given were heavily seasoned with fable and myth, they often contained more than a grain of truth.

More or less contemporary with these theological poets were the first mathematicians. These were the first to construct rigorous and sustained arguments which arrived at necessary conclusions about quantity. Next came the philosophers of nature, who are widely regarded as the first true philosophers. For these men did not present their accounts in terms of symbols or myths but rather in the form of carefully reasoned arguments.[2]

The first such account of the natural world of which we have any record comes from Thales of Melitus, a Greek from the sixth century BC. Recognizing that in order to make sense of

[2] Supplementary text: Thomas Vernor Smith, *Philosophers Speak for Themselves: From Thales to Plato* (Chicago: University of Chicago Press, 1956), chapter on the Pre-Socratics.

something, it is necessary to understand it in terms of its simplest parts, elements, and causes, Thales posited that the whole of nature was reducible to a single material cause: water. The variations of shapes and forms which are found in the natural world, Thales argued, could be explained by the process of rarifying or compacting water. While the modern student may find such an account laughable, we should not be too quick to dismiss such an explanation. To do so would be to miss the essential insights which later led to more refined discoveries. In fact, if one considers the matter carefully, water seems to be a good first guess as the ultimate material principle of the universe. Water is the most abundant element on the surface of the earth, covering nearly three quarters of the earth's surface. All living things depend upon water, so it seems to be a principle of life. Moreover, water takes the form of a solid when it freezes and a gas when it is heated.

After Thales came a number of other philosophers of nature. Some of these, like Thales, posited a single material principle as the ultimate principle of existing things. For example, Heraclitus posited fire as this ultimate principle, since it most of all seems to be a principle of change, and the world of nature which we observe is constantly in motion. Some other philosophers, considering that a single principle did not seem sufficient to explain the complexity of natural things, posited multiple principles. For example, Empedocles posited four elements: earth, water, air, and fire, which were either brought together by love or torn apart by strife. Still other philosophers, such as Anaxagoras, considered that the various substances which we observe in the natural world were not reducible to one another, and so he posited an unlimited number of principles which were tiny particles found in each thing. Whatever particle predominated in a given substance, say a piece of gold, was what that substance appeared to be (i.e., it looked like gold because it had more gold particles than anything else). Anaxagoras also posited a kind of mind which was separate from these other particles, and which separated them and brought them together to form various substances.

While each of these philosophers seemed to be in disagreement about the ultimate explanation of the world of nature, a brief investigation of their positions shows a common thread in their accounts: All of them posit some material principle or principles as the underlying substance of all things, and each of them posits some kind of moving force by which these material principles may be moved from one state to another contrary state. That is, all agreed that there is a common material principle under everything and a force that moves this matter.

In this respect, these first philosophers seem to have anticipated some of the claims of modern physics, which, although mathematically sophisticated in its description of these forces and principles, nevertheless provides fundamentally the same account: a single material element (such as a quark), which is combined with or divided from others by opposing forces. We shall consider whether or not an account of reality which posits only material principles as the causes of natural things is tenable in our course on natural philosophy.

CHAPTER 2

What Is Philosophy?

Before considering what philosophy is, it may be helpful to dispel some false notions or characterizations about philosophy. Often, when the modern student thinks of philosophy, he imagines some kind of esoteric theory which has very little to do with the real world. University humanities departments are filled with courses on various philosophers and philosophies, nearly all of which are opposed to one another, and most of which seem to have very little relation to the world in which we live. Often it is asserted that the widespread disagreement among philosophers is a sign that philosophy is not a true science but rather a matter of choice or preference. After all, mathematicians, physicists, and chemists have no problem agreeing on what is true about their respective subjects; surely this is the sign of authentic science.

Whatever the student's preconceived notions may be about philosophy, let us set them aside for now and consider: What did philosophy mean in its original sense? What did it mean for those first philosophers?

For the first philosophers, philosophy had everything to do with the world in which we live. After all, the first philosophers were attempting to give an explanation of this world in terms of its beginnings, causes, and elements. The starting points of all philosophy were the common experiences had by all men: the experiences of motion, of substances both living and non-living, and of man and the various communities in which he found himself—the family and the citystate. Each of these things is complex and difficult to understand. And so the task of philosophy was to discover what was most basic in each of these experiences. That is, the role of philosophy was to explain these various and complex experiences in terms of their principles, causes, and elements.

It is important to note that it is *common experiences*—that is, experiences capable of being shared by *all* men[3]—which serve as the starting point of philosophy. In this sense, philosophy is not concerned with personal experiences or preferences. These personal experiences, while they may be important for the life of an individual, cannot be the subject of rational discourse and investigation insofar as they are personal. Therefore, philosophy, since it takes its starting point from common experiences, is firmly rooted in certain and obvious experiences verifiable by anyone who seeks to investigate the matter in detail.

From the foregoing, we can formulate a provisional definition of philosophy: philosophy is an explanation or account—that is, a setting in order—of the causes of reality.

But does philosophy consider every cause of reality? For instance, does a philosopher concern himself with the cause of the cake rising in your mom's oven? Certainly there is a cause there, but the philosopher does not seem to be primarily interested in this kind of a cause. Rather, the philosopher interests himself

---

[3] We note an exception for those who have some defect, such as men born blind. For such men, color can never be a subject of knowledge, since, due to a material defect, they can never experience the nature and properties of color. The same may be said of those lacking any other sense from birth.

principally with the ultimate and most universal causes of reality. For example, Thales was seeking the first causes of all substances and motions. So we might refine our definition of philosophy as an account of the *ultimate* causes of reality.

But doesn't the theologian investigate the ultimate causes of reality too? Yes, but he does so by consulting the sources of divine revelation. The theologian takes, so to speak, God's perspective, which is more universal even than the philosopher's perspective. So to distinguish philosophy from theology, we should add that philosophy is an account of the ultimate causes of reality *according to human reason*. That is, philosophy considers reality insofar as it can be known by human reason alone, without the help of faith in divine revelation. We shall take this as our definition of philosophy throughout this course.

Now let us consider some of those objections in light of our definition of philosophy. First, can it be truly said that there are many philosophies? Surely there can be many accounts of the causes of reality, but not all of them fit the facts. Those accounts of the causes of reality which do not actually explain reality, but explain it away or distort it, are false accounts. They do not actually represent the true causes of reality, and so they are false philosophies. And since reality is one thing, there can only be one true account of the causes of reality. Therefore, while there may be many false philosophies, there is only one true philosophy. And a philosopher is a good philosopher to the extent that he hits upon this true philosophy, and he is a bad philosopher to the extent that he fails to provide a true account of the causes of reality. What then is the ultimate measure of a good philosopher? Common experience. When all is said and done, every philosophy must measure up against the yardstick of reality: a reality readily accessible to all diligent investigators.

But why is it that there is so much disagreement among philosophers, while we find scientists so much in agreement? First of all, it is necessary to distinguish the areas in which there is agreement and disagreement. Scientists, such as physicists and chemists, are, by and large, in agreement about certain things such as the particular measurable and reproducible results of various experiments. It is easy to get someone to agree that when you heat water to one hundred degrees centigrade at an air pressure of fifteen psi, it begins to boil. Philosophers are also in agreement about such things; for example, they agree that living things are in some significant way different from non-living things, and that motion is obvious to the senses. But both the philosopher and the scientist often disagree with their fellow colleagues about what the *true causes* are of these things which are manifest in their particular science. A survey of the recent physical theories from Newton to Bohr to Einstein to Heisenberg reveals a radical disagreement about what are the true and ultimate causes of physical phenomena. It is in the realm of the ultimate causes of common experiences where philosophers disagree as well. And so, in this regard, philosophy is no different from the applied sciences.

There are other reasons, however, why we often find more disagreements among philosophers than among scientists even in the area of ultimate causes. For one thing, philosophy deals with the most universal causes of all reality, while physical scientists usually restrict themselves to a more limited scope, such as the causes of chemical reactions. It is inherently more difficult to arrive at the more universal causes than it is to arrive at more particular causes; for example, it is easy to identify the cause of *this* horse—namely, its two parents—but it is a very difficult thing to identify the cause of horse in general. Therefore, philosophy requires a much broader experience, more careful investigation, and a longer time before these causes can be determined. It is not surprising then that it is easier to be deceived in the realm of philosophy than in the experimental sciences since the former is more difficult. Finally, since philosophy is so universal, many of the conclusions of philosophy bear upon what is good and bad in human actions. For example, if I discover through philosophy that a man is only perfected through actions under the guidance of reason, then this indicates that those human actions which are performed contrary to reason (under the control of emotion or passion) are evil. On the other hand, if I discover that the interior angles of a triangle are equal to the sum of two right angles, this will have no bearing on anyone's moral life. And so, in the area of philosophy, a bad will can be an impediment to arriving at truth: A man sometimes will not accept a conclusion simply because he doesn't want to, not because the evidence isn't conclusive. On the other hand, in mathematics and the experimental sciences, the will plays little or no part, so it cannot be a source of disagreement.

In summary, philosophy is an account of the ultimate causes of reality according to reason. There is only one true philosophy since reality is one as reflected by the common experiences accessible to all. The disagreements among philosophers that are not found to the same degree in scientists are not a sign that philosophy is not a rigorous science; rather, they indicate that philosophy is very difficult, that it requires much study and experience, and that the student of philosophy must be morally upright.

CHAPTER 3

A Roadmap to All Things Knowable[4]

Let us now broadly consider the whole body of knowledge. That is, let us consider all the various sciences and arts—everything that can be known—and show how they are related to one another. This will be our "roadmap" for the rest of this course since it will lay out all the different subjects which we will study this year, in addition to some other subjects which will have to wait for later. (A chart of this roadmap is shown in *Figure 1* on the following page.)

If we are going to draw a roadmap of all the things that can be known, we have to determine what makes something knowable. Well, one thing that is essential in order to know something is that you need to be able to distinguish it from other things. When something is hidden or mixed up with other things, it can't be known until you separate it out. We even use the word *confused* to indicate that we don't know something since things which are confused are not distinct. So in order to know something, it must be distinct from other things.

But not only must something be distinct from other things, it must also have some definite relation to other distinct

[4] Supplementary text: Thomas Aquinas, *Commentary on the Nicomachean Ethics*. I.1.

Order
Order discovered by Reason
Order produced by Reason
Order revealed to Reason which is…
Sacred Theology
Speculative Sciences
Practical Sciences (Arts)
Exists in matter but defined without matter which is…
Mathematics
Exists in matter and defined with matter which is…
Natural Philosophy
Exists without matter and defined without matter which is…
Metaphysics
Order Produced in the Soul
Order Produced outside the Soul which is…
Material Arts
Order Produced in reason's own act which is…
Logic
Order Produced in the act of the will which is…
Ethics

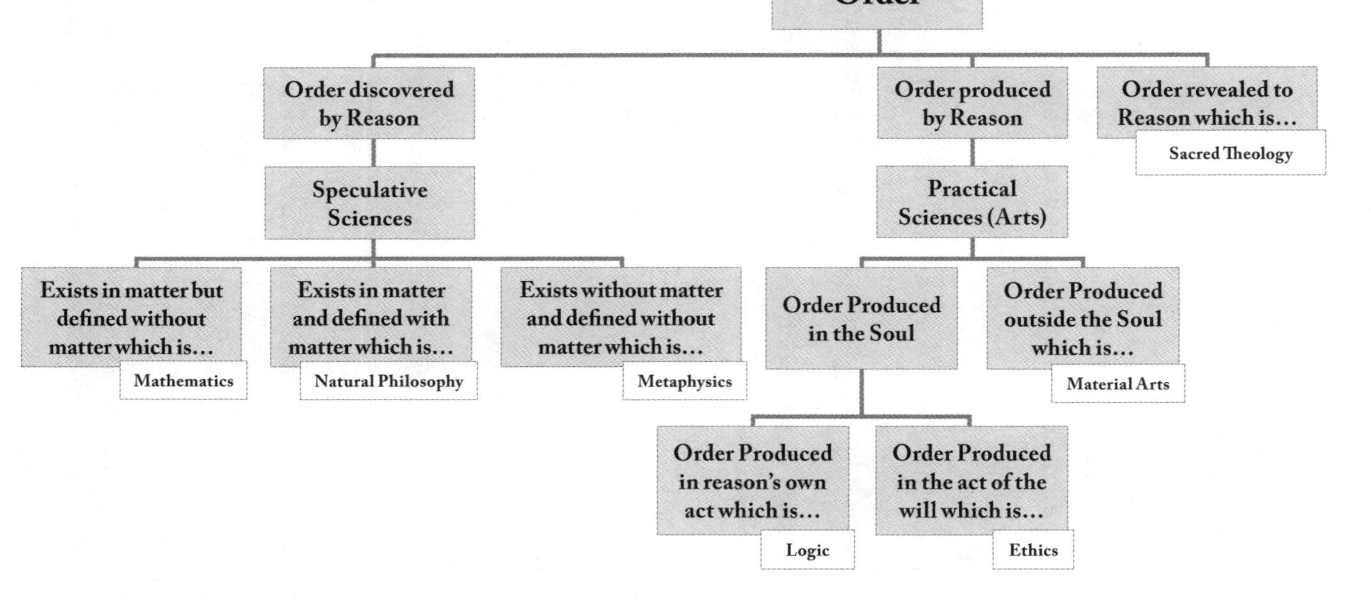

Figure 1

things. Let's take an example. Suppose I want to know how many people are in a classroom. What will I have to do? If there are a lot of students there, I have to count them. But in order to count them, I have to be able to distinguish them (if the classroom is too dark, I will not have much success). Next, I have to be able to relate them so that one is before another (I count this student first, then that student second, and so on until I am done). If I don't order them in some way, I may end up counting the same student twice, and this will not do.

So, for something to be known, two things are necessary:

1. There must be some distinction between things.

2. There must be some definite relation between the distinct things.

When distinct things have a definite relation to one another, then there is an *order* among them, and this order is the foundation of all knowledge. In summary, everything which can be known has an order.

Now, there are three general kinds of order which men can consider.

First, there is an order which our reason (the human mind) discovers in things. For example, as we are looking at nature, we find some caterpillars. We take them home and put them in a jar. After a while, the caterpillars make cocoons, and eventually butterflies emerge. As often as we do this, the same order is kept: we notice that butterflies always start out as caterpillars. So we discover that there is an order between caterpillars and butterflies: caterpillars come first, and butterflies come later. We may also observe that boys always come before men. After enough examples, we might even draw a more universal conclusion: in living things, the immature or the imperfect always comes before the perfect. This is an order which our reason discovers in things.

Second, there is an order which reason puts into things. When a boy builds a tree house, he assembles all the pieces of wood. Then he nails them together into a certain shape; it might even have a roof and some windows. This is not an order which the boy discovered in the tree or the wood; it's an order which he put there. Take another example: when a child learns how to speak, he first uses words indiscriminately. But he eventually learns how to order his words into meaningful sentences. He has put order into his speech. Eventually, he may study grammar, which is the art of ordering speech and writing. So this second kind of order is the order which reason puts into things.

There is a *third* kind of order as well, and it is a very special case. It is the order which God reveals, or shows, to man. Not everything that can be known can be discovered or produced by man. Some things are so great and high that man is unable to make them or even to discover them on his own. Now, the greatest thing of all is God (as we shall later argue), and certain things about God are so beyond the human mind that man could never discover them unless God Himself told us about them; for example, man could never have figured out that there are three Persons in God unless God Himself revealed this. So this is a third order, and the science which studies it is called Sacred Theology.

In summary, everything which can be known has an order. But order is related to human reason in three ways:

1. The order which reason discovers in things (considered in the *speculative sciences*)
2. The order which reason produces (considered in the *practical sciences*, also known as the *arts*)
3. The order which is revealed to reason by God (considered in *sacred theology*)

So this is the beginning of our roadmap of knowledge. There is a three-pronged fork in the road which leads to the various branches of knowledge. Leaving aside the road which leads to sacred theology, let us consider the road to the speculative sciences in more detail.

First of all, when we call a science "speculative," we do not mean "speculative" in the sense that it is uncertain. Sometimes we speculate about future events, or things which we cannot know, but this is not what is meant by the term "speculative" in "speculative science." The English word "speculative" comes from the Latin word "spectare," which means "to look at." When someone looks at something, he does not do anything to it; rather, it does something to him. The spectator is one who simply beholds or watches something, without affecting it or changing it in any way.

In the same way, there are certain types of things which we simply behold, but we do not do anything to change or affect the order which we see in the thing which is known. When the first astronomers looked at the heavens, it was not with the purpose of changing or affecting the motions of the stars and planets. It was simply to know the order in these motions. When we study nature, we do not make natural things to be what they are. They were what they are long before we ever came on the scene, and they will remain what they are long after we have gone. We may well alter a natural thing; for example, we might heat sugar and make caramel. But to make caramel is not the same thing as to make caramel be what it is. On the other hand, it is by human art that a desk or a chair or a house is what it is. Such things did not exist before man made them, and their very definitions have their origins in the human mind. In short, the thing that makes a speculative science different from a practical science is that the purpose or end of speculative knowledge is *truth*, while the purpose or end of practical knowledge is *making or doing something*. The reason for a recipe is solely practical, but to know that the diagonal of a square is commensurable with its sides is the kind of knowledge which is for the sake of truth.

It is true to say that speculative knowledge is useless. But this is a compliment, not an insult. When something is useful, it is always useful for something better than itself. A business partnership is useful for gaining money, so the money is more desirable than the partnership. And money is desirable for obtaining other goods which are pleasant or noble, such as good food or a good education. A pile of money which is never used is no better than a pile of sand. So, since everything useful is not as good as the things for which they are used, the best things are those which are not useful for anything else. This is the case with speculative knowledge: it is useless in the sense that it is desirable for its own sake, not for the sake of anything else.

Let us now divide up the kinds of speculative knowledge. Some things are material—that is, they exist in matter—and are defined or understood with matter. For example, a tree is material, and its definition would include its matter—namely, wood. The science which considers these things is called *natural philosophy*. Some things are found to exist in matter, but when we define them or consider them, we do not define or consider them with matter. So, for example, a triangle is something which I first observed in some material thing, such as a metal triangle, but when I define a triangle in mathematics, I do not include any particular matter in its definition. I simply say that it is a closed figure having only three straight sides; it is as if I simply ignore the matter when I define "triangle" as such. The science which considers these things is called *mathematics*, which includes both geometry and arithmetic. Now, if it could be shown from human reason that there are things which are immaterial (that is, they do not exist in matter), then this could be the subject of a third speculative science: the science of things which do not exist in matter, nor are they defined with matter. This science is called *metaphysics*. The fourth logical possibility (namely, things which are immaterial and defined with matter) does not correspond to anything in reality, so there is no branch of speculative science corresponding to it.

In summary, the speculative sciences are divided into

1. natural philosophy, which considers things that exist in matter and are defined with matter,
2. mathematics, which considers things that exist in matter but are defined without matter, and
3. metaphysics, which considers things which exist apart from matter and are defined without matter.

Let us now consider the practical sciences. The most obvious practical sciences, or arts, are those which put order into external matter. Architecture puts order into wood, stone, and metal to form a building; electrical engineering puts order into wires and components to form circuits and other electrical devices; sculpture puts order into marble and clay and metal to form statues, and so on. But it is also possible to put order not only into external materials but also into one's own soul. For example, we can order our thoughts, our desires, or our actions. Therefore, the arts can be divided into two general categories:

1. Perfective arts, by which a man puts order into the acts of his soul

2. Material arts, by which a man puts order into external matter

The first category includes arts which are perfective of man himself, so we call them the perfective arts. The second category includes arts which do not perfect man as such but impose forms upon material things outside of man, so we call them the material arts.

Since man has reason (that is, the part of his soul which allows him to understand what is true or false) and a will (that is, the part of his soul which allows him to choose what is good or evil), it follows that there are two kinds of acts which a man can order within his own soul: the acts of reason and the acts of the will. The art which a man uses to order the acts of his reason is called logic, while the art which a man uses to order the acts of the will is called ethics. The word "ethics" is used here in a broad sense which includes all the ways in which a man can order the acts of his will. The aim of ethics is to make a man good. But since man naturally belongs to a family and also some kind of civil society, there are other branches of ethics which consider how to make a man a good family member or a good member of society. We will consider ethics in the final quarter of this year.

CHAPTER 4

Logic as the Art of Arts

We have just seen that logic is an art (that is, a practical knowledge) which a man uses to put order into the acts of the part of his soul that we call reason. The aim of the remainder of this quarter will be to acquire the principles of this art of logic. Very few things are more useful and desirable than this since logic is the art of arts. That is, logic is directive and, so to speak, king over all other arts.

What do we mean when we say that logic is the art of arts? First, we need to have a definition of art. *An art is a fixed and certain procedure, established by reason, by which human acts reach their due ends by appropriate means.* The key part of this definition for our purposes is that an art is something established by reason. Only human beings have art. Other animals make things, but always in the same way, by instinct. When a spider spins a web, it's always the same kind of web for a given species of spider. But when a man builds a building, it can look like the Empire State Building or Saint Peter's Basilica. The product of human art can have any variety of shapes and sizes because it is the work of reason, which sees a multitude of possible forms that it can put into a given material. So, since every art is something established by reason, the art which perfects reason itself must, in some way, be the highest art of all. It is one thing to know how to think well about a particular subject, like managing a business; it is a much greater thing to know how to think well about every subject. This is just what logic aims at: it aims at perfecting the acts of reason.

In short, *logic is the art of reasoning well.*

So logic helps us to reason well. But we reason about things we know. Therefore, logic is about the things we know. But is it about all the things we know? Take the following two statements:

1. I know that the angles within a triangle sum to 180 degrees.

2. I know that I am cold right now.

Is the word "know" used in the same sense in these two statements?

In the first statement, the word "know" seems to refer to a kind of intellectual knowing: a knowledge of something universal, which is always true of all triangles not just this one, here and now. In the second statement, the word "know" seems to refer to a kind of knowledge in the realm of sensation: a knowledge of something particular, which is true here and now but might change later. It is important to distinguish between sense knowledge and intellectual knowledge. Logic is concerned with intellectual knowledge since it is the art by which reason is strengthened. Logic does not help us to know better through our senses.

Sense knowledge is never the conclusion of an argument; intellectual knowledge is. To know that I am cold, or that I see this tree, or that I hear this sound is something I know immediately without an argument. Once it is sensed, it is known. But I must use an argument to prove that the interior angles of a triangle sum to 180 degrees, or that the human soul can exist apart from a body.

Whenever we reason, we reason from some statements which we already know (we call these statements premises) to a statement which we do not know (we call this statement a conclusion). Therefore, when we say that logic is the art of reasoning well, we mean that it is *the art of habitually reasoning to true conclusions from true premises.*

Here, a question naturally arises: Is all intellectual knowledge the conclusion to an argument?

Let us suppose that it is. Well then, how do we know that the conclusion of an argument is true? By knowing that the premises are true. But how will we know that these premises are true if all knowledge is the conclusion to an argument? In order to know that the premises to the first argument are true, they will have to be the conclusion of other arguments. But these other arguments will also have premises, and so on to infinity. It is like the story of someone who believed that the world was at rest on the back of a giant elephant. When he expressed this position at the lecture of a philosopher, the philosopher asked him, "If the world is only at rest because it is held up by a giant elephant, then what is holding up the elephant?" To which he responded unfazed, "The elephant is being supported by a giant turtle." "But," continued the philosopher, "what is holding up this turtle?" He thought pensively and finally said, "Oh no, sir, you will not catch me in your argument: it's turtles all the way down!"[5] One who holds the position that all intellectual knowledge must be the conclusion of some argument is in the same ridiculous position, but instead of turtles, it's premises all the way down!

---

[5] A version of this story is told about an exchange between William James and a guest at his lecture by the linguist John R. Ross (*Constraints on Variables in Syntax*, 1967).

In other words, if we assume that everything which we know must be proved by an argument, we must conclude that we know nothing at all. But this is absurd; therefore, there must be some truths which we know without having to prove them through an argument or else there can be no reasoning at all. There must be foundational truths that do not need to be proved by an argument. We call these truths "self-evident" truths.

CHAPTER 5

Some Difficulties and Questions about Logic[6]

Before we begin examining this art of reasoning well, we must first answer two questions. First, is logic really necessary? Second, even if logic is necessary, is it possible to have an art of reasoning well?

One reason for thinking that logic is not necessary is that most people seem to get along fairly well without overtly using it. It seems that we rarely, if ever, use it in conversations. Moreover, many people are successful scientists, businessmen, teachers, and so forth without having ever taken logic. So it seems that we do think fine on our own: thinking seems to come naturally to us. To this objection, we reply that logic is not necessary for thinking, but for thinking *well.* To take an analogy, let us say someone was an athlete in a sport where physical strength was an important element. He may be able to play that sport well at a low level, like high school, just by his natural abilities without ever doing any exercise or weight training to increase his strength. But at a certain level, if he wants to get better, he will have to resort to exercise and weight training. Nature needs to be helped by art if one is to perfect his abilities. Logic is like exercise or weight

6 Supplementary text: *The Meno* by Plato.

training for the mind. As long as the subjects we think about are sufficiently particular and close to the sensible, there is little difficulty in reasoning accurately. But when the subjects become more difficult and universal, we find that we make many mistakes in our thoughts.

At the highest levels of thought, in philosophy and theology, the man who has not strengthened his mind by means of logic is virtually helpless. He's like a wrestler competing in a weight class much higher than his own. We might also draw an analogy between logic and a telescope. So long as the things we are looking at are sufficiently close to us, we can depend upon our natural power of sight. But when the things we are looking at are very distant, our natural abilities need to be enhanced by something artificial: a telescope. For us, sensible things are very close to us, but the causes of these things (especially the most universal causes) are very far away. Logic is like a telescope for the eye of our minds: It allows us to perceive things which are far away more clearly. This is one reason why there are so many disagreements among philosophers; many of them simply haven't fully acquired the art of logic, so they fall prey to many mistakes that they can't even see. In summary, logic is necessary if we are to reason *well* about *difficult* matters.

So let us grant that logic is necessary in some sense. But is logic even possible? Let us put the question more concisely: Whenever we come to know something which we do not know, we come to know it from something we already know.[7] In this sense, logic can

[7] For example, I can't come to know the area of a rectangle unless I already know the length of the sides of that rectangle. The fact that we always come to know new knowledge from something we already know is also illustrated by the fact that a student learns through examples, which are better known instances of the thing we come to know through the example.

be defined as *the art of coming to know what you do not know through what you do know*. But how is it possible to discover something which you do not already know? Socrates presents this difficulty in the *Meno*:

> **Meno**: But how will you look for something when you don't in the least know what it is? How on earth are you going to set up something you don't know as the object of your search? To put it another way, even if you come right up against it, how will you know that what you have found is the thing you didn't know?
>
> **Socrates**: I know what you mean. Do you realize what you are bringing up is the trick argument that a man cannot try to discover either what he knows or what he does not know? He would not seek what he knows, for since he knows it, there is no need of the inquiry, nor what he does not know, for in that case, he does not even know what he is looking for.[8]

Think about the following questions, and discuss it in class (if possible): What is the difficulty Socrates presents in *Meno* with trying to discover something which you do not know? What is the solution to this difficulty?

Even granting that we can in fact come to know things from things we already know, there is still another problem: How do we know that it is possible to improve our capacity for arriving at truth by means of some art like logic? Perhaps there is no set method which can be used to strengthen our minds, or perhaps there is no rhyme or reason to the mistakes we make. Perhaps they

[8] The Dialogues of Plato: *Meno*, 80 d-e.

are unavoidable no matter what we do. In the end, the answer to this question is relatively simple.

It is possible because, if we examine the kinds of mistakes we make when we reason about things, we realize that we generally tend to make the same kinds of mistakes. For instance, many times we make a mistake in an argument because we use a word in two different senses without knowing it, which is called equivocation. Take the following example: All men ought to seek to be happy, but taking drugs makes some men happy. Therefore, some men ought to take drugs. In this argument, the word "happy" is taken in two different senses—namely, "happy" means the good which perfects human nature in the first sense, and "happy" means a particular physical pleasure in the second sense—and so the argument does not follow.

What is true about equivocation is also true about many of the other mistakes we make in reasoning: they are often the same *kinds* of mistakes. Since we make the same kinds of mistakes in our reasoning, there can be some definite and fixed procedure (that is, an art) of looking for and avoiding these mistakes. In other words, so long as there are regular mistakes we make, there can be regular methods of fixing those mistakes. And a regular method of fixing mistakes in our reasoning fits the definition of logic as an art of reasoning well.

So, logic is both possible and necessary. And it is the most useful and beneficial of all the arts. Let us now consider this noble art in detail.

CHAPTER 6

The Acts of Reason Studied in Logic[9]

When we say that man is different from the other animals because man is rational while the other animals are non-rational, what do we mean? What is it that most obviously sets apart a rational being from one which is non-rational? Is it the fact that man has an opposable thumb or that he walks upright that makes him rational? When we watch a sci-fi movie like Star Wars, some of the non-human creatures depicted are obviously rational, while others are clearly not. But what is the thing that makes us think that this creature is rational while that one is not? The bottom line in most cases, the thing that tells us for certain whether or not this or that outer space creature is rational, is whether they can speak, or at least communicate in some way.

Speech is the most obvious sign of rationality.

Moreover, since it is what is most known to us, speech is the key for understanding the activities of our own reason. We express the hidden thoughts of our mind through our words so that our words help us understand our thoughts better. Words are sensible signs of our invisible thoughts. Shakespeare expresses this well in the words of Miranda to Caliban: "I pitied thee, took pains to make thee speak, taught thee each hour, one thing or other; when thou

[9] Supplementary text: St. Thomas Aquinas, *Proemium to the Posterior Analytics*.

didst not, savage, know thine own meaning, but wouldst gabble like a thing most brutish, *I endowed thy purposes with words that made them known*."[10]

There are essentially three things we do when we speak: name, state, and conclude. First, we name things; then we make statements about the things we name; and finally, by putting statements together, we conclude other statements from them. In fact, these three things are the first three human acts ever recorded. We read in Genesis 2 that God brought the various animals to Adam to see what he would call them: "The man gave names to all the cattle, and to the birds of the air, and to every beast of the field" (v. 20). So the first thing Adam did was name things. The next time Adam speaks is when God brings Eve to him, and he says, "This at last is bone of my bones and flesh of my flesh" (v. 23). So the second thing he does is make a statement about some of the things he has named—namely, bones and flesh. Finally, Adam draws this conclusion: "She shall be called Woman, because she was taken out of Man" (v. 23). So the third thing Adam does is give a reason for a new statement which he has concluded from the things he said before.

Now, corresponding to the three things we do in our speech, there are three acts of our reason. We use the first act of our reason when we *understand the things we name*. For example, I understand what a triangle is by defining it as a closed figure with only three straight sides. This naming of things helps us come to know things as they exist—a good definition tells us what something is that sets it apart from everything else, while a bad definition misses the mark on what precisely sets this thing apart from all the others.

[10] William Shakespeare, *The Tempest*, Act 1, Scene 2.

We use the second act of reason when we *understand the true or the false*. Statements which affirm or deny that something is so are true or false. When we say that "this is that" (for example, as when we say that man is an animal), then we are putting two things together in our thoughts. When we say that "this is not that" (for example, as when we say man is not a rock), then we are dividing two things from one another in our thoughts. When we put together two things in our thoughts which are together in reality, or when we have divided two things in our thoughts which are divided in reality, then we have made a true judgment. On the other hand, when we have put together two things in our thoughts which are not together in reality, or when we divide two things in our thoughts which are together in reality, then we have made a false judgment.

Finally, the third act of reason involves *coming to know or guess a statement from other statements*. This last activity of coming to know or guess statements from other statements is what we typically call reasoning in the most proper sense, since it includes and presupposes the other two acts of reason. Reasoning is related to understanding as motion is related to rest. When we understand the meaning of a word in the first act, or we understand the truth or falsity of a statement in the second act, there is no movement in our thoughts. But when we reason, we first consider one statement, and then another, until we finally arrive at a conclusion. So we move from one statement to another. This is a reason why the third act of reason is better known to us than the first and second acts of reason: as Shakespeare says in *Troilus and Cressida*, "things in motion sooner catch the eye than what not stirs." Just as it is easier to notice a deer running through a field rather than one that is standing still, so too do we notice the movements of reason from one statement to the next more easily than we can give a compact definition of a word.

So there are three distinct acts of our reason. For this reason, there is a part of logic dedicated to each of these three acts: the art of defining, the art of understanding a statement, and the art of syllogizing. Let us see how these three parts of logic can help us to reason well.

We have already seen that the ultimate purpose (or end) of logic is to perfect our reasoning power. Our reasoning power will be perfected when we are able to know conclusions perfectly, or at least as perfectly as the subject matter allows. When we form an argument which causes us to know a conclusion perfectly, we call this argument a *demonstration*. Thus, a demonstration is the most perfect kind of argument, and all logic is ordered to constructing demonstrations. Since a demonstration is a kind of argument, let us take a concrete example of an argument.

Every complete argument has at least two statements. A statement which is used in an argument is called a premise. If a statement necessarily follows from two premises, this statement is called the conclusion of the argument. The conclusion is not so much a *part* of the argument as an *effect* of the argument. The premises are like parents while the conclusion is like the offspring of the premises. The following is an example:

(Premise) All numbers divisible into two equal parts are even.

(Premise) But the number 1032 is divisible into two equal parts.

(Conclusion) Therefore, 1032 is an even number.

In this argument, how are we going to be certain that the conclusion is true? There are two things we need to know to determine conclusively whether or not the conclusion of this argument is necessarily true: we need to know (1) that the premises are true and (2) that the form of the argument is good. In the following argument, the conclusion follows necessarily from the premises, but it is false because one of the premises is false:

All trees have roots.

All roots are groundhogs.

Therefore, all trees have groundhogs.

Is it possible for a true conclusion to follow from false premises? Yes, but not *because* of those premises. If we replace the word "groundhog" with the word "branches" in the above syllogism, then we arrive at a true conclusion which follows necessarily from the premises, but this conclusion is not true *because* of those premises. The fact that branches grow on trees is not because roots are branches, but for some other reason. Thus, it might happen by chance that a true conclusion will follow from false premises. But in such a case, this argument would not contribute to our knowledge of the conclusion. Logic considers how to determine whether a premise is true in the part of logic called the art of understanding a statement; moreover, logic considers how to determine whether a conclusion follows because of the premises in the part of logic called the art of syllogizing.

But let us suppose now that the premises are both true; this is still not enough to guarantee that a true conclusion follows. In the following argument, the form is not good, so nothing necessarily follows from it:

All squares have four sides.

All trapezoids have four sides.

Although one might be deceived into believing that all squares are trapezoids, this conclusion would not follow necessarily from this argument. The reason is not because the premises are false (in fact both premises are true). The reason why no conclusion follows is that the argument does not have the right form. Logic considers what constitutes a good form of an argument and a bad form of an argument. This is also done in the part of logic called the art of syllogizing.

But if we are ever to determine whether or not a statement is true, we must know the meanings of the words used in that statement. Logic helps us to understand the meanings of words by defining them. This is done in the part of logic called the art of defining.

In summary, the art of logic has three principal parts:

1. The art of defining

2. The art of understanding statements

3. The art of syllogizing

The *art of defining* helps us to understand the words, or terms, in a statement. Knowing the meanings of the terms makes it possible for us to determine, in the *art of understanding a statement*, whether or not a given statement is true when we join or separate words in a statement. Finally, knowing whether or not the statements (which are premises in an argument) are true makes it possible for us to determine whether or not the conclusion is true, and this is done in the *art of syllogizing*.

CHAPTER 7

The Art of Defining

(A) "What's in a Name?"

Whenever we define something, we use names. As we saw earlier, a name (or a word) is something men use to express their thoughts in a sensible way. A name can be defined as *a vocal sound which signifies by agreement, and which does not have any part that signifies by itself.* Let us now explain each of the parts of this definition. A name is first of all a *vocal sound* (written names are signs of spoken ones, so the vocal sound is primary). But is a name just any vocal sound? No, a vocal sound must *signify* something to someone if it is to be a name, otherwise it is just gibberish, as when a baby makes sounds imitating speech. What about screams or groans or the cry of a baby? These seem to signify something. But a scream or a groan or a baby's cry all signify something naturally. No matter what language you speak, you know what they mean. So a name is a vocal sound that signifies *by mutual agreement*. That's why you have to learn a language; it's not something natural or instinctual.

Now some vocal sounds have parts which, taken by themselves, signify something. For example, "I run" has two parts which each signify something by themselves. But the vocal sound "run" is a name since, although it has parts (the letters *r*, *u*, and *n*), *none of its parts means something by itself.* Sometimes a name may have parts which, if pronounced separately, have signification but do not have the same signification when they are parts of that name. For example, the vocal sound "forgiving" has parts "for" and "giving." But insofar as they are parts of this one name "forgiving," they do not signify anything separately. (To take another example, the word "pineapple" does not signify a pine and an apple.) However, if the same sounds were pronounced separately in a statement such as "gifts are for giving," then each would be a name in its own right.

Since we use names whenever we define things, definition presupposes names. Therefore, names are better known to us than definitions. This means that, simply speaking, a definition does not make us understand a name (since we already must have some understanding of the names that we are defining beforehand). Rather, definitions help us to understand a name *better or more perfectly.* To take an example, we have a name like circle. We understand in a sort of vague or confused way what this name means, and we are easily able to point out examples of circles. But when we define a circle as "a closed figure in a flat plane having all its points equidistant from a center point," then we have a more distinct understanding of what a circle is. Therefore, a definition is speech signifying distinctly what a thing is. This is like a tool which the mind uses to acquire a more distinct and clear understanding of a name it already understands.

The Univocal Names Used in Definition: Genus, Species, and Difference

Names are used either univocally or equivocally. When a name is said of many things with the same meaning, then it is used univocally. For example, when I say "animal" of dog, cat, and horse, the name "animal" has the same meaning in each case. But when a name is said of many things with different meanings, then it is used equivocally. For example, when I say "bat" of a wooden club and also of a flying mammal, the name "bat" has two different meanings. When a name is used univocally, it is often called a "univocal name." When a name is used equivocally, it is often called an "equivocal name." Of course, the same name can be used both univocally and equivocally in respect to different things. The name "bat" is used equivocally when said of a flying mammal and a wooden club, but it is used univocally when it is only said of the flying mammals.

When a univocal name is said of many things which are different in kind, then this name is called a *genus*. In the above example, the name "animal" is a genus, since the things of which it is said are different kinds of things. A dog is a different kind of thing than a cat, and so on.

When a univocal name is said of many things which differ only as individuals but are of the same kind, then this is called a *species*. So, the name "man," which is said of Bob, Jim, Susan, and so on, is a species. In a looser sense, a species can be the name of any particular kind of thing placed under a genus. So, for example, the name "bird" can be called a species in relation to its genus, animal, but in relation to "canary" and "sparrow," it is a genus. Thus, in this looser sense, the same word can be both a genus and a species.

There is also another kind of univocal name. When we wish to add something to a genus to narrow the genus to a particular species, we use a *difference* (sometimes called a specific difference). For example, in order to get to the species "man" from the genus "animal," we must contract or narrow the meaning of the genus "animal" using the difference "rational." Usually, we need multiple differences to get to a species. For example, to get to the species "square" from the genus "quadrilateral," we add the differences "equilateral" and "equiangular." Thus, a difference can be understood as the name which separates species under the same genus. Or, understood another way, the difference is a name said with one meaning of many things which signifies *how they are what they are*. This implies that not any specifier will make an appropriate difference. For example, red, white, and blue are not different ways of being a triangle, because color has nothing to do with what a triangle is. Rather, one must look to what a triangle is in order to determine the appropriate species-making difference. Since a triangle is a three-sided figure, and having all sides equal, two sides equal or no sides equal are different ways of being three-sided, then the appropriate division of triangle into its species will be equilateral, isosceles, and scalene.

Every perfect definition is composed of (1) a genus and (2) a species-making difference. Therefore, the art of defining will consider two things: both how to find the right genus and how to find the right difference to arrive at the definition of the name signified by the species.

The Kinds of Definition

But here a question arises: When we define, do we define things or names? Put another way, is a definition of a thing or is a definition of a name? In practice, we define both and in separate ways. Sometimes, a definition simply indicates what the name means, but other times it indicates what a thing is. The former merely describes what we intend to signify with our words, while the latter says distinctly what some existing thing is. In total, there are three types of definitions which we will discuss: nominal definitions, essential definitions, and definitions by property.

Let's look at some examples to help us understand the differences between these definitions.

When I say that a mermaid is an animal with the head and torso of a woman and the tail of a fish, I am simply saying what the name means. There is no thing corresponding to the name. A definition which only gives an account of what the name means is called a *nominal* definition. On the other hand, when I say that a man is a rational animal, I am signifying what a man is, not just what the name "man" means. When my definition actually signifies the very essence or "what it is to be" of a really existing thing, then it is called an *essential* definition. Often, a nominal and an essential definition can be given for the same name. For example, the name thunder can be defined as "a rumbling noise in the clouds" (nominal definition) or as "the sound produced when air expands rapidly due to being superheated by lightning" (essential definition). Besides nominal and essential definitions, there are also definitions by properties. A definition by property does not signify what a thing is in the strict sense of the word, but it does indicate a real thing in terms of something which is better known to us. For example, we can define a dog as an animal with four legs which barks. Or we can define man as an animal with the ability to laugh. Both essential definitions and definitions by properties are definitions of things, while nominal definitions are definitions of names only. The best definitions are essential definitions; the definitions by properties are second best; and the nominal definitions are better than no definition at all, even if they tell us very little. An essential definition is better than a definition by properties since it is better to know something through its causes than merely through its effects: the causes of a thing tell us more than its effects. And both essential definitions and definitions by properties are better than nominal definitions because essential definitions and definitions by properties signify what an existing thing is, while there is no guarantee that a nominal definition will signify anything in reality.

Definitions of Complete and Incomplete Things

Another way in which we can distinguish kinds of definitions is based upon the different kinds of *things being defined*. This is different than the distinction into definitions which are essential, by properties, and nominal: those are three *different ways* of defining the *same thing*. But here we are considering how *different kinds of things* result in different kinds of definitions. Sometimes the things we define are *complete* things, like a man or a horse. In these cases, every part of the definition signifies what these things are. For example, a man is a rational animal: both "rational" and "animal" somehow signify what a man is. But sometimes the things we define are *incomplete* things, like an arm, or a color, or a soul. These incomplete things do not stand on their own. They must be understood in reference to something else outside of them upon which they depend. Therefore, when we define incomplete things, part of the definition is from outside of the thing itself. For example, an arm is a limb *of a body*; a body is not what an arm is, but it is what an arm is *in*. Again, a color is a quality *of a surface*; a surface is not what a color is, but it is what a color *is in*. Again, a soul is the principle of the life *of a body*; a body is not what a soul is, but it is what a soul *is in*. In each case, when we define an incomplete thing, we include its proper subject in the definition, but the proper subject is in the definition in a significantly different way than the other parts of the definition. The other parts of the definition signify the essence or "what it is," while the proper subject does not.

Definition of a Thing and the Four Marks of a Good Definition

Let us now define "definition."

Things are definite, as opposed to vague or confused, when we clearly see their limits or boundaries. We say that a photograph has high definition when all the boundaries of the things in the picture are clearly visible. A bodybuilder has definition when the boundaries between the various muscle groups are clearly visible. In a similar manner, a definition of a thing sets off the boundaries of that thing so that it is set apart from all other things in our mind. In short, we grasp what the thing defined is, as distinct from all other things. And since definitions are expressed first in speech, we can say that *definition is speech signifying distinctly what a thing is*. Notice that we are obviously talking about definitions of things, not just nominal definitions.

From our definition of a definition, four marks or characteristics of a good definition follow:

First, since definition concerns what a thing is, a definition must be of *some existing thing*; for that a thing exists is presupposed to it being of this or that kind. If a thing doesn't exist, it doesn't have a real nature or "what it is to be." I mean by "existing" those things which actually exist and those things which are able to exist. Thus, we may have a definition of a table or we may have a definition of a million sided regular polygon, but we could not have a definition of a square circle. Why? A table exists actually (actual existence) and a million-sided regular polygon is able to exist (potential existence), while a square circle is not able to exist in any way since the combination of the notions "square" and "circle" implies a contradiction.

Second, a definition must be *coextensive with the thing defined*. For when we are to signify exactly what a thing is, we are required to say what that thing is and only that thing, nothing more and nothing less. Moreover, since a definition must signify *distinctly*, we must first say what is common to all things so named, and then say what common thing is proper to all things so named. Hence, definitions take the form of genus/specific difference since the genus signifies what is common while the specific difference signifies what is proper. Therefore, every definition must include at least two names. Take a triangle, for example. If we were to say that a triangle is a closed figure in a flat plane, this would not clearly set "triangle" off from everything else in our mind, since circles, squares, and the like are all closed figures in a flat plane. On the other hand, if we were to add that a triangle has only three equal sides, this would be too narrow, since some things which are triangles have unequal sides. Therefore, our definition of triangle will be correct only if we include in our definition everything which all triangles have and nothing which no triangles have. The definition "closed figure in a flat plane with only three, straight sides" is common to all triangles and can be applied to nothing else except triangles.

Third, a definition should give *an account of the cause* of a thing defined or something essentially related to that cause. There are four types of causes that can help us understand what it is that we are defining: formal, material, agent, and final. When one asks the question "what?" one is primarily seeking the *formal cause* (thus, we define "form" as *that cause which makes a thing to be what it is*). For example, "a closed line in a single plane which is equidistant at all points from a center point" would be the shape, or formal cause, of a circle, and would also constitute the definition of a circle. Other than formal cause, there are three other kinds of cause. *Material cause* is that from which a thing is made and which is in it (like marble, which is in a statue). *Agent cause* is the first source of a thing's motion (like a pool player who causes the motion of the cue ball). *Final cause* is that for the sake of which something is or comes to be (as when a desire to be healthy is the cause of a man jogging). These other kinds of causes may also enter into a proper definition. Sometimes all four causes are in a single definition, as when we define a bookcase to be "a manufactured article used for storing books, comprising a solid material with a frame and shelves." Here we find an account of the four types of cause: (1) agent causality, since the bookcase is manufactured by some (presumably human) agent; (2) final causality, since the bookcase is made for the sake of storing books; (3) material causality, since the bookcase is made from some solid material (e.g., wood, metal, etc.); and (4) formal causality, since the bookcase is shaped to have a frame which holds shelves. Again, marriage can be defined as the stable union of a freely consenting man and woman for the generation and education of children. See if you can identify all four causes in this definition of marriage.

Although, most properly, a definition gives an account of the cause, sometimes when we ask what a thing is, we seek simply to set the thing apart from other things in our mind (in this way, for example, man is set apart from the other animals by the definitions "featherless biped" or "the animal with speech"). Thus, we may also define (i.e., limit or set the bounds of) a thing according to its properties since these are essentially related to the cause of the thing and serve to set the thing apart from all other things.

Fourth, since a definition signifies, it is a sort of teaching or instruction. Thus, *the defining terms must be better known than the term defined*, otherwise there is no instruction. Now, things are better known to us in many ways. For instance, "better known" may mean that which is more perfectly known, as when we say that mathematics is better known to our teacher than it is to us. Furthermore, that which is better known may signify what is closer to the senses, since knowledge first comes through the senses. Better known may also mean that which is more familiar, as when we want to tell someone what a stranger looks like, we might say, "John, who you do not know, looks like our friend Bill." Finally, better known may indicate that which is most certain. For instance, when we see a man coming over the hill in the distance, it is first known to us that there is something on the hill, then it is apparent that it is some kind of animal, then it becomes known to us that it is a man, and finally we are aware that it is our friend Joseph. Thus, it is more certain, or better known to our sensation, that Joseph is a substance, and after that an animal, and after that a man, and after that the man Joseph. In other words, that which is more universal, or general, is better known in this sense. It is in this final sense that the defining terms of a proper definition are better known than the word defined, since this sense of better known relates to what the thing is. However, it is in the second and third sense (i.e., that which is more familiar or closer to the senses) that we define according to properties to set the thing defined apart from other things in our mind.

Thus, in summary, we can say that there are four marks of a good essential definition:

1. It must correspond to an existing thing.
2. The defining terms must be coextensive with the term defined.
3. It must give an account of the cause or causes of the thing defined.
4. It must use terms which are better known than the term defined.

These four marks can be used to test any *essential* definition to see if it is a good definition or not. However, if the definition given is not essential, but rather is a definition by properties, then only marks 1, 2, and 4 apply. And if the definition given is only nominal, then only marks 2 and 4 apply. This is why essential definitions are best, followed by definitions by property, and then finally nominal definitions. Now that we have laid out what a definition is and the kinds of definition, let us proceed to determine how we can actually discover definitions.

(B) The Ten Categories[11]

We saw above that every definition has a genus. Therefore, the first thing we should do in formulating a definition of a thing is determine or discover what genus it falls under. Aristotle was the first man to discover the ten categories. These ten categories are the ten highest genera. Thus, since a genus is a name said univocally of many things different in kind, the ten categories are ten *highest* names which are said univocally of many things different in kind. Since these are the ten highest genera, everything that exists can be defined in terms of one of these. These ten categories are *substance, quantity, quality, relation, when, where, acting upon, undergoing, position, and outfit.* Examples of these are man, horse, rock (substance); a meter, seventeen (quantity); hot, green, sweet (quality); double, larger, fatherhood, alike, unequal (relation); ten o'clock, yesterday (when); in the classroom, on the beach (where); hitting, burning, cutting (acting upon); being hit, being burnt, being cut (undergoing); seated, standing, lying (position); armored, shod, shirted (outfit).

Let us look at each category in detail so that we can more easily determine what category a given thing should have as its genus.

---

[11] Supplementary text: Aristotle: *The Categories.*

Substance

Substance is the first category. It is being in the primary sense of the word, because all other beings are dependent upon substances. For example, when we ask a question about quantity—"how much?" or "how many?"—we are asking "how much sugar," or "how much fabric," or "how many people," or "how many hamburgers." Sugar, fabric, people, and hamburgers are all substances; we are asking "how much of this something" when we are looking for an answer to the question of quantity. Again, when we speak of quality, we presuppose a substance: there is no such thing as white or hot or sweet all by itself, but there is such a thing as a white car, a hot plate, sweet syrup, etc. We can show this to be true for each of the other categories as well. For this reason, we can see why the name "substance" comes from a Latin word meaning "to stand under," because substances stand under all the other categories of being. For their part, the other nine categories are all called "accidents." They are not accidents in the sense of a car accident or something which happens by chance, but they are accidents in the sense of a being which exists in another. "Accident" comes from the Latin word meaning "to fall to," or to happen to belong to. An accident doesn't belong to itself; it always belongs to and exists in another thing. Thus, a substance is that which does not exist through something else, while an accident is that which exists through, or is present in, a substance. Moreover, a substance is not said of anything else. Rather everything else is said of substances. For example, in the statement "this sugar is white," I say white of this sugar. But I don't say this sugar of something else.

Substances can be individual (like John, or Mary, or this rock, or that dog, Fido) or universal (like man, or rock, or dog). Often, individual substances are called primary substances, while universal substances are called secondary substances. Primary substances are the foundation of secondary substances; the primary substances are substances in the truest sense of the word, and they seem to be more real than secondary substances. What do we mean by this? We can only understand secondary substances (rock, dog, man) by first experiencing primary substances. Primary substances are what we first sense and know, and thus we come to the more universal knowledge of secondary substances only after our encounter with a primary substance.

Additionally, secondary substances are said of primary substances, and some secondary substances can be said of other secondary substances, but primary substances are not said of anything else. What does this mean? Let us take an example. We can say that man is an animal (animal is said of man) and that Socrates is a man (man is said of Socrates), but we can't say that Socrates is of anything else. The only thing we could say that Socrates is himself (that is, saying "Socrates is Socrates"), in which case we are not really saying anything at all but just repeating the name Socrates.

Because every definition uses universal names (names said of many things), primary substances do not have a definition since each primary substance is a unique, particular individual thing (e.g., Socrates the man, Fido the dog). Therefore, only secondary substances can be defined. There is a definition of man, but not of *this* man. There is a definition of bookcase, but not of *this* bookcase. Nevertheless, we can say what *this* man is: he is a rational animal, but this is not *his* definition, since he has this in common with all other men. There is no difference which we can assign to separate him from all other men, other than giving accidents which have nothing to do with what he is in himself as a substance.

There are six marks which can help us to identify whether a given thing is a substance or not. These marks are characteristics belonging to substances:

1. A substance is not in an underlying subject.

2. For secondary substances, the name of the substance and its definition are said of an underlying subject. For example, when we say that Paul is a man (secondary substance), we can also say that Paul is a rational animal (definition of that secondary substance). But when we say that Paul is brown, we cannot say that Paul is the definition of brown—namely, that Paul is a kind of color.

3. Primary substances seem to signify a "this something"—that is, something which both exists on its own and is complete in its nature.

4. There is nothing contrary to a substance. White is contrary to black and virtue to vice, but nothing is contrary to dog.

5. A substance cannot be more or less of what it is. There is no gradation in whether or not something is a substance—it either is that substance wholly or it is not it at all. For being a substance, there are no intermediates between "is" and "is not." One man may be shorter or lighter than another, but he is not less of a man. A Chihuahua is as much a dog as a Great Dane.

6. The mark most proper to substance is that it can change in such a way as to receive contraries and yet remain one in number (i.e., it can remain the same individual). For the same individual can at one time be sick and another time

be well, or at one time be dark and at another time light, and the same man can at one time be vicious and another time virtuous.

Quantity

Something in the category of quantity answers the question "how much?" or "how many?" Some quantities are continuous, like length or surface or volume, while others are discrete, like number. Continuous quantities have a common boundary. For example, two lines meet in a point, two surfaces meet in a line, and two volumes touch at a surface. There is a specific, set position where a common boundary or limit is shared. But discrete quantities do not have a common boundary. For example, what are the parts of the number ten? In one way, the parts of ten are five and five, but in another it can just as truly be said to be three and seven, or eight and two; furthermore, these numbers do not touch one another or form a boundary with one another. Sometimes, students are used to seeing numbers represented on a number line, but this is misleading since a number is something measured by an indivisible unit, and is not some continuous quantity. What we mean by "number" here corresponds to the notion of positive whole integers.

Further distinctions also must be made. Not everything which we call big or small is a quantity. For example, we say that World War II was a big war, and that there is a lot of white in that room. In these cases, what we really intend to signify is that World War II involved a large *number* of people or that it took place over a long *time* or that it took place over a large part of the earth's *surface*. And when we say that there's a lot of white, we mean that the *surface* in which the color white exists is large.

There are three marks which help us to identify things in the category of quantity.

1. There is nothing contrary to a quantity.

For example, there is nothing contrary to a foot or to a surface. If someone were to say that many and few or large and small are contraries, he is really considering them as relations, not as quantities. For nothing is called large or small in itself, but only in relation to something else. It makes perfect sense, for example, to call a mountain small and a grain of sand large if they are referred to things of the same kind.

2. A quantity cannot be more or less than what it is.

For example, a pound of feathers is not less of a pound than a pound of bricks, nor is one two-foot length more than another two-foot length. Certainly, one quantity can be more than another, but this is not the same as saying that a quantity can be more or less than *what it is.*

3. It is most proper to quantities that they can be called equal and unequal.

Relative Names

A name or thing is relative (toward another) when it has in its very notion that it is toward another thing. For example, a parent is always the parent of a child, and a child is always the child of a parent. Again, a double is always the double of a half, and a half is always the half of a double. A master is the master of a servant, and a servant is the servant of a master. In each of these cases, there is always a second term toward which the other is referred.

Some names are relative according to the way in which we speak about them, but they are not relative in their very being. For example, we may speak of a habit *of* something or knowledge *of* something. Habit and knowledge are not relative in the strict sense of the word. Rather, they are qualities. But since a relation is founded immediately upon these qualities, we speak of them as if they were relative. But a double and a half or a father and a son are relative in their very being. That is, in their very definition, they are toward the other so that you couldn't understand one without at the same time understanding the other. In the very notion of what it is to be a half, there is included the notion of double. This is not true for things like habit and knowledge or the other relatives which are only relatives according to the way we speak.

There are three marks which can help us to identify things in the category of relation in the strictest sense (things relative in their very being). 1) Things relative in their very being reciprocate naturally in speech. When I say "right," you say "left." When I say "double," you say "half," etc. But when I say "page," it takes a while before you can come up with something that sounds relative (like "paged" as in a book is paged—that is, something having pages). So page and paged thing, or wing and winged thing would not be relative in their very being but only in our way of speaking. 2) Things relative in their very being exist together by nature. The one can't be unless the other one exists. For example, double cannot exist unless its half exists. 3) Things relative by nature must be thought of together: they are understood in a determinate way together and even somehow defined in reference to one another. And this must be true in both directions. For example, I cannot determinately understand something to be double without also understanding in a determinate way that which is its half. But I can understand virtue without vice, and I can understand sight without understanding blindness, even though blindness cannot be understood without sight.

Quality

A quality is that in virtue of which something is said to be of one kind or another.[12] For example, an apple is said to be a different kind of apple than another apple in virtue of their colors (e.g., red or green). Color is a quality since it is that in virtue of which an apple (for example) is said to be of one kind or another.

There are four main kinds of quality:

1. Habits and dispositions
2. Natural abilities
3. Affective qualities
4. Figures or shapes

Habits and dispositions differ in that habits are more long lasting and durable, while dispositions are more temporary and more easily changed. Justice and temperance are examples of habits since they are firmly established qualities of our soul by

[12] An added precision is helpful here. Sometimes we distinguish kinds of things based upon accidental differences, like black and white, or square and round. These are accidental qualities. However, there are also specific differences (considered earlier in this chapter when we treated the univocal names used in definition). For example, the specific difference for man would be "rational," and a specific difference for dog would be "four-footed," and the specific difference for bat would be "winged." These specific differences which determine the kinds of substances there are look and sound like qualities, but they are more properly put in the category of substance since they signify how a substance is what it is. So we might say that there are accidental qualities and substantial qualities. At this point, we are considering accidental qualities.

which we act in a particular manner (i.e., justly or temperately). Any firmly established, acquired quality through which someone or something acts in a determinate way can be called a habit. Examples of dispositions are sickness, health, grumpiness, or kindness. These things are not as permanent as habits: a man might be healthy one day and sick the next, or grumpy one minute and kind the next.

Natural abilities are like habits, but they are not acquired in any way; rather, they seem to be part of someone's or something's natural constitution. For example, we speak of someone being a natural runner or swimmer. Or we say that someone is ruddy or that someone has a sickly constitution.

Affective qualities are qualities which can affect other things in such a way as to produce some kind of effect or motion in those other things. These qualities are all sensible qualities since they produce an effect in our senses. For example, sweet and bitter, hot and cold, black and white are all affective qualities.

Figures and shapes are also qualities, such as straight or curved, or oblong or round. Thus, for example, a line is said to be of one kind or another in virtue of its shape.

There are three marks which can help us to identify things in the category of quality:

1. Qualities have contraries. For example, white is contrary to black and just is contrary to unjust.

2. Some qualities can be more or less what they are. An example of this is that white can be more or less white, since a white thing can become whiter.

3. It is most proper to qualities that they are said to be similar or dissimilar—a color is similar to another color, or a shape is similar to another shape.

Acting Upon and Undergoing

These two categories obviously go together. Things which are acting upon something are causing an effect in something else. Things which are undergoing are receiving some effect from an external cause. For example, heating is a kind of acting upon, and being heated is a kind of undergoing. Teaching is a kind of acting upon, while learning is a kind of undergoing. Both acting upon and undergoing admit of contrariety and more or less. For example, heating is contrary to cooling. Again, heating admits more or less, as when we say that this fire is heating more than that one, or this person is pleasing me more than that one.

Where

Those things which are in a place are said to be somewhere. "In the Lyceum" was the where of Socrates, and "in Orange County" is the where of Saint Michael's Abbey. Thus, whenever a term designates the way in which something is by reason of its place, this term belongs to the category of where.

However, the category where should not be confused with place, which is a species of the category of quantity. Thus, if I were to ask what is the *place* of the peanut butter, you would answer "the inside surface of the jar" (and surface is a quantity). But if I were to ask *where* is the peanut butter, you would say "in the jar" (which signifies a where but not a quantity). To take another example, if I want to find a place to put my new sofa, I should consider how big a place it is. If the place is smaller than my sofa, my sofa will not fit. It makes perfect sense to ask the question "how big of a place do you have?" since place is a measurable quantity. But does it make any sense to ask the question "how big of a where do you have?" or "how much where do you have?" No. Where something is merely tells you that something is *in* a place. It does not consider the "how much" of the place itself. So where is not a kind of quantity, while place is.

Position

Positions, such as seated or standing, add the notion of an order of parts in a place to the notion of where. So everything in a position has a "where," and not only that, but there is a definite relation of the parts of the thing. When a person is standing, his parts are all in line straight up. When a person is sitting, some parts are vertically oriented (his torso and lower legs) and others are horizontally oriented (his upper legs).

When

A name signifies something in the category of when if it signifies at what time or in what time a subject exists. When did Socrates exist? In the fifth century BC. When is dinner? At six o'clock. Notice that although *when* and *time* are very closely related, *when* is not the same as *time*. The relation between when and time is like the relation between where and place. When I say "How much time did that take?" and you answer "Two hours," the answer "two hours" is a time which is measurable and answers the question "How much?" And therefore, time is in the category of quantity, since quantities answer the question "How much?" or "How many?" But if we indicate that something is either in a span of time or at a moment in time (for example, "at three o'clock"), this does not answer the question "How much?" but rather answers the question "When?" It makes no sense to ask the question "How much when do you have?" But it makes perfect sense to ask the question "How much time do you have?" since time is a quantity and when is not.

Outfit

This last category of being is unique to man. All other animals have by nature the tools they need for survival and acting. Some animals are equipped with claws and fur, or wings, etc. But man, because of his power of reason, has so many diverse activities which can help him to attain his end that no single set of natural tools could adequately equip him with everything he needs. So man makes by art what other animals have by nature. And so it happens that, unlike the other animals, man must fashion clothes for himself as protection, and it is natural for man to have some outfit in all lands, times, and cultures. Man is naturally outfitted. This gives rise to the unusual and ephemeral category of *outfit*. Names such as shirted, armored, clothed, costumed, and shod signify beings in this category. Things in this category can be found in animals when man clothes them for his own use or enjoyment, as when a horse is armored.

Leading Things Back into a Genus

After consulting your experience of reality, you will soon discover that many things do not easily or obviously fit into the ten categories described above. For example, into what category would you place a point, or growth? Into what category would you place blindness or "not-red"? Many things do not fit perfectly within a category, yet they can be led back into a category because they have a determinate relationship to things that do fit neatly and perfectly within one of the categories. Let's take the examples we just listed. Into what category would you place a point? Well, a point doesn't have a size, nor does it answer the question "How much?" So it doesn't seem to fit perfectly into the category of quantity. Nevertheless, a point does seem to be a principle of the category of quantity, so we can lead it back to quantity: it belongs with quantity, but less perfectly than things like lines and surfaces. How about growth? That seems to belong to the category of quantity too. But again, it is more properly a change or increase in quantity than quantity itself. Growth seems to share imperfectly in quantity, to have quantity in an unstable way. Yet we can lead growth back to the category of quantity, so long as we understand that it belongs in that category in an imperfect way. Something similar may be said about blindness and "not-red." If we were to define them, we would begin by using the categories into which sight and red fall, respectively. Sight seems to be a natural ability (the second species of quality), while red falls in affective quality (the third species of quality). So we can lead blindness (which is a lack of sight) and "not-red" (which is the negation of red) back into the category of quality. Blindness and "not-red" do not fit perfectly into quality, but they do have a definite relationship to things that do fit perfectly in the category of quality, so we lead them back to that category.

In summary, we can say that something can be led back into a category if that thing is:

1. A principle of things in that category (like a point),

2. Some imperfect mode of things in that category (like growth),

3. A lack of something in that category (like blindness), or

4. A negation of something in that category (like "not-red").

(C) Getting from the Genus to the Species

Let us summarize what we've learned so far about the art of definition.

(1) First, we have seen that whenever we define, the definition has at least two parts: the *genus* and the *difference* or *differences*. When the genus and the differences are put together, they form the *species*. For example, the species *man* is formed from the genus *animal* and the difference *rational*; and the species *square* is formed from the genus *quadrilateral* and the differences *equiangular* and *equal-sided*.

(2) Second, we have seen that there are several kinds of definitions: nominal definitions, essential definitions, and definitions by properties.

(3) Third, we have noted four marks of a good definition (it must correspond to an existing thing; the defining terms must be coextensive with the term defined; it must give an account of the cause or causes of the thing defined; and it must use terms which are better known than the term defined).

(4) And finally, we have learned the ten categories which are the highest genera in terms of which everything else can be defined (*substance*, *quantity*, *quality*, *toward another*, *when*, *where*, *acting upon*, *undergoing*, *position*, and *outfit*).

Knowing the ten categories can help us to discover the genus which should be in a thing's definition. But the genus is only a part of the definition. We need to be able to find the whole definition. The following three sections will be useful for discovering the whole definition of something.

Wholes and Parts

A definition is a whole which has parts. But when we use the names "whole" and "part," do we always mean the same thing by these names? Let's look at the following argument. *Animal* is a whole which includes *man* as one of its parts since the term "animal" includes man as well as ox, cat, dog, and all the other animals. On the other hand, *man* is a whole which includes *animal* as one of its parts, for *man* is *rational animal*: animal is part of the definition of man. Thus, in the former, animal (the whole) is greater than man (the part), yet in the latter, man is greater than its part animal. So it seems to follow that animal is greater than itself. Does this argument follow? Of course not, but what is the fallacy? The fallacy is an equivocation on the words "whole" and "part" because there are different meanings of each.

One meaning of "whole" is an *integral* whole. This is the meaning of "whole" which is best known to us, and we tend to think of all wholes and parts in this way. For example, a house is an integral whole, and wood and bricks are its integral parts. Again, a triangle is an integral whole, and each of its sides is an integral part. A word (cat) is an integral whole, and its letters (c, a, t) are its integral parts. A definition is an integral whole and the genus (animal) and difference(s) (rational) are its integral parts. In the case of an integral whole, the whole is simply equal to the sum of its parts. But there is another kind of whole. Let us look at the example of triangle. On the one hand, I could say that triangle (integral whole) can be divided into three straight sides (integral parts). But I could also say that triangle is divided into equilateral, isosceles, and scalene. In this case, we are treating triangle as a *universal* whole, not as an integral whole. A universal whole includes its parts but not only that; *the universal whole can be said of each of its parts* since it is understood to be in each of them. Although equilateral is a part of triangle, I can also call it a triangle. But this is not true of an integral whole and its parts. I cannot call one of the sides of a triangle a triangle. The same is true of names like animal and bird. Not only are falcons, sparrows, and ostriches parts of bird, they can all be called birds. But I can't call the wing of a bird a bird, since a wing would be an integral part of bird. So there are two meanings of the word "whole": integral and universal. There is a third meaning of "whole" as well, called a *potential* whole. The potential whole is somewhat between an integral whole and a universal whole. The potential whole contains its parts in power or ability, just as the ability to lift two hundred pounds contains the ability to lift one hundred pounds. We will consider this kind of whole when we take up the study of the soul in third quarter.

Thus we have three meanings of the word "whole":

1. Integral (the whole is simply equal to the sum of its parts)
2. Universal (includes its parts but also can be said of each of its parts)
3. Potential (contains its parts in power or ability)

Division and the Four Kinds of Opposites

If we are going to get from a genus to a species, we need to be able to divide a genus into its parts. Every division is based upon some kind of opposition. For example, when a family is divided into a husband and wife, this division is based upon the opposition between male and female. Again, a family can be divided into parents and children. This division is based upon the opposition between begetting and being begotten. When oil is divided from water, this is because of the opposition between the light and the heavy (oil is light and water is heavy). When God will divide all men at the last judgment, this division will be based upon the opposition between good and bad.

Let us apply this principle to the category of substance. Substance can be divided into material substances (bodies) and immaterial substances (angels). And material substances can be divided into living and non-living. And living material substances can be divided into sentient (animals) and non-sentient (plants). Finally, sentient living material substances can be divided into rational (man) and non-rational. So we have reached the definition of man by dividing the genus of substance all the way to the species man.

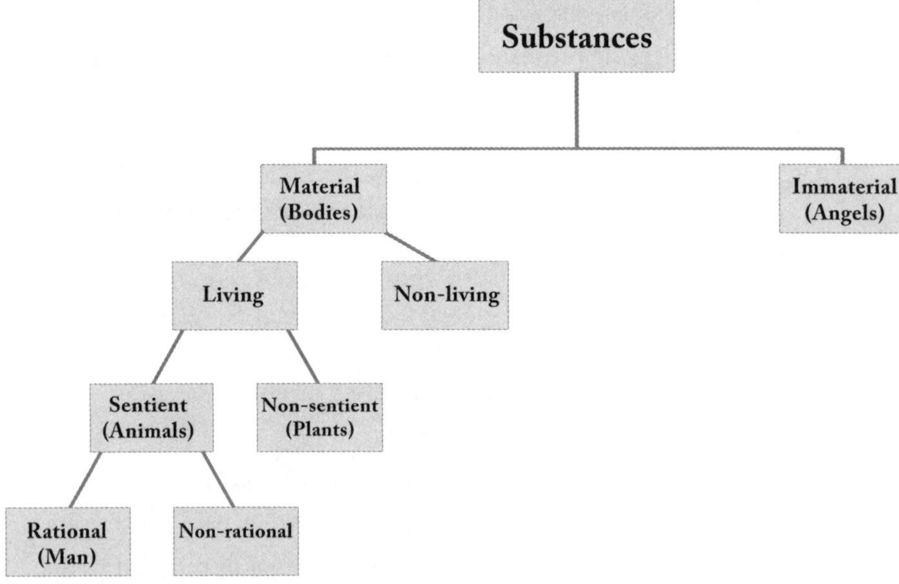

Figure 2

From these examples, we see that it is important to know about the kinds of opposites if we are going to be able to divide a genus into its parts and arrive at the definition of the species.

There are four ways in which things can be opposed: correlatives, contraries, having/lacking, and affirmation/negation. Some things are opposed as *correlatives*, such as double and half, begetter and begotten, and knowledge and what is known. Some things are opposed as *contraries*, such as white and black, virtue and vice, and knowledge and error. Some things are opposed as *having/lacking*, such as blindness and sight, light and darkness, and knowledge and ignorance. Finally, some things are opposed as *affirmation/negation*, such as man and not-man, colored and not-colored, and knowledge and not-knowledge.

We can show that the correlatives are least opposed while the affirmations/negations are most opposed. Correlatives are opposed, but in such a way that they have to exist together at the same time. If there is a half, there has to be a double. Contraries are more opposed than correlatives, since contraries do not exist together. Nevertheless, contraries must be of the same kind (that is, they must be in the same genus). So white and black are in the genus of color, virtue and vice are in the genus of habit, etc. Having/lacking is more opposed than contraries since things which are opposed in this way are not even in the same genus. Nevertheless, things which are opposed by the opposition of having/lacking must be in the same kind of subject. For example, only an animal capable of sight can properly be called blind (rocks or trees are only called blind in a metaphorical sense). Finally, affirmations/negations are most of all opposites, for things which are opposed in this way have nothing at all in common.

Least Opposed	**Correlatives**	**Exist together at the same time in the same genus and the same kind of subject**
↓	**Contraries**	**Do not exist together, but exist in the same genus and the same kind of subject**
↓	**Having/Lacking**	**Do not exist in the same genus, but exist in the same kind of subject**
Most Opposed	**Affirmations/Negations**	**Nothing in common at all**

Of these four kinds of opposition, contraries are the most important for the logician, since they are the opposites farthest apart *in the same genus*. And the logician is interested in how he is going to divide a genus into its parts.

The Main Senses of Before and After

Once a logician divides up his genus, he needs to be able to set in order the things under that genus to arrive at a complete definition. For example, we can define man as a rational animal. Here "animal" is the genus and "rational" is the species-making difference. In the English language, the more universal term (the genus) usually comes last, while the more specific terms of a definition (the species-making differences) are listed before the genus. Thus, it would be out of order to say that man is an animal rational. Let's take another example. Which seems to be the more correct definition: (1) A triangle is a three-sided figure or (2) A triangle is a figure sided-three? The first seems more correct, even though the same differences are used. Why? Because the order of the terms is better in the first definition. Before something can have sides, it must be a figure, and before something can have three sides, it must have sides. Having sides comes before having three sides. This leads us to a consideration of the ways in which one thing can be before or after another thing.

There are four main senses in which one thing can be before another, and a fifth sense related to one of the four chief senses. *First*, one thing can be before another thing *in time*. For example, your father and mother existed before you in time. *Second*, one thing can be before another thing *in being*. For example, one can exist without two, but two cannot exist without one. Thus, one is before two in being. *Third*, one thing can be before another thing *in our knowledge*. For example, I must know animal before I can know rational animal. Or I know what a right triangle is before I know the Pythagorean Theorem about right triangles. *Fourth*, one thing can be before another thing *in goodness or nobility*. For example, man is before the other animals in nobility, and we would choose a good sculpture before a bad sculpture because it is better. There is also a fifth sense like the second sense; namely, one thing can be before another as a cause is before its effect. For example, the act of moving is before the act of being moved, even though both the moving and being moved happen at the same time. This sense of before and after is different from the second sense because the cause and the effect reciprocate, whereas that which is before in being does not reciprocate with that which is after in being. Of these five senses, the second, the third, and the fifth will be especially useful for defining.

Let's take an example which puts this tool of before and after to work. Try to define gold. In the definition of gold, we should indicate both that it is a metal and an element. But which of these comes before the other? Is gold a metallic element or an elemental metal? Look now at the second sense of before and after. Which is before in being: metal or element? Element is before metal since elements can exist without metals existing, but metals cannot exist unless elements exist. So element is more fundamental and universal, which makes it the genus in the definition. Therefore, we should define gold as a kind of metallic element. We could add something like "yellow in color" to get a more complete definition: gold is a yellow-colored, metallic element.

The Three Roads to Definition

This is the moment we've all been waiting for. Once the student has all the above-mentioned tools at his disposal, he is in a position to actually construct definitions. There are three roads one can follow to arrive at a definition. We can come to a definition from above (that is, from more universal terms), from below (that is from less universal terms), and from all sides (that is, from equally universal terms). Each of these roads starts from something better known to us.

Sometimes that which is more universal is better known to us. For example, it is obvious that a virus is a substance, and even that it is a body, but it is not as clear whether or not it is a living body. In this instance, substance and body are better known to us than living body, since an understanding of living body presupposes an understanding of substance and body.

Sometimes that which is less universal and closer to our senses is better known to us. For example, we know *this* tree (one we can see and feel) better than tree universally. Again, we know what the cause of this man is (his mom and dad) better than we know the cause of man universally.

Finally, sometimes that which is an equally universal effect is known better than its cause. For example, we know that man is capable of speech better than we know the cause of this—namely, the fact that man is rational. Again, we know that a lunar eclipse is a shadow cast on the surface of the moon before we know the cause of this—namely, the interposition of the earth between the sun and the moon. Let us now look at examples from each method.

Definitions from Above

We have already seen how to arrive at the definition of man from above—namely, by dividing the category of substance until we reached the definition of man. Let us look at one more example: the definition of a square. When we come to the definition of a square, we start with the category of quantity and then proceed to divide through contraries until we arrive at the definition of a square. First, we must divide quantity into continuous/discrete. Next, divide continuous into line, surface, and volume. Next, divide surface into flat and curved. Next, divide flat into figures with straight sides/curved sides. Next, divide straight-sided figures into those with three sides, four sides, etc. Next, divide four sides into equilateral/not equilateral. Finally, divide equilateral into right angled/non right angled. Since it is normally not convenient to express the definition of a thing with all of its superior genera, usually only the proximate genera are used, as when we say a square is an equiangular, equal-sided quadrilateral.

Definitions from Below

Let us attempt to define *dog* by approaching the definition from something less universal (namely, particular kinds of dogs). A Great Dane is big, has short hair, four legs, a tail, and it barks. A Chihuahua is small, has short hair, four legs, a tail, and it barks. A Sheepdog is medium sized, has long hair, four legs, a tail, and it barks. So all of these kinds of dogs have four legs and a tail, and they all bark. So we can define dog as the animal with four legs and a tail which barks. What kind of definition is this?

The same thing can be done with triangles. A scalene triangle has three unequal straight sides. An isosceles triangle has three straight sides, two of which are equal. An equilateral triangle has three straight sides, all of which are equal. Therefore, what is common to all triangles is that they have three straight sides. Therefore, triangle can be defined as a figure with three straight sides.

Definitions from All Sides

We can also arrive at an essential definition from things equally universal to the definition—namely, from the properties of a thing. Aristotle does this in the beginning of his book on metaphysics. There, he gives six properties of a wise man, and he reasons from these properties to the definition of wisdom. The wise man (1) knows all things, (2) can give an account of the cause and can teach others, (3) is more certain, (4) knows difficult things, (5) knows the best things, and (6) directs other things. So wisdom must be the kind of knowledge by which the wise man does all these things. But someone who knows the first causes of all things can do all six of the aforementioned things. Therefore, wisdom must be a knowledge of the first causes.

Again, man is an animal who can speak, who can choose between opposites, who can appreciate humor, who can produce artifacts, etc. But all these things belong to one who can grasp the order among things. Therefore, man is the animal who grasps order—that is, a rational animal (the word "rational" comes from the word "ratio," which means order or proportion).

These are just a few examples of the three roads to definition. The student should appreciate that he need not restrict himself to only one of these roads when approaching a definition. Sometimes, more than one of these roads should be followed in order to arrive at a single definition. For example, someone might take the road from below to arrive at the genus of man (animal), and then might take the road from all sides to arrive at the specific difference of man (rational).

Special Cases

Every once in a while, when trying to define something, we run into a special case that needs extra thought. One such special case that comes up very often is when we are trying to define artificial things rather than natural things. Unlike natural things, artificial things are not fully one. Their matter is something natural, but their shape or form is something artificial, something imposed from outside. Take a simple case of a pipe carved from wood. The matter of the pipe is something natural: wood. But its shape was put into it by a man carving the wood. The shape of a pipe is not a result of some internal inclination of the wood to shape itself into a pipe. It comes completely from outside, from the agency of a man. Therefore, when trying to define a pipe, we are actually trying to define *two* things, not *one* thing. From the standpoint of its matter, a pipe is a substance (wood), but from the standpoint of its outward form, a pipe is a quality (the fourth species of quality: figure or shape). Therefore, with all artificial things, one must define it in both ways: you must define its form and then the matter it is in. The definitions of artificial things will therefore fall into *two* categories, and this should not be surprising, since in reality you are defining *two* things. However, often in such cases, one can simply give "artifact" as the genus of the definition, which signifies that the thing being defined is not naturally one thing. Let's take an example to illustrate: A city is something man-made. From the standpoint of its matter, a city can be defined as something along the lines of "many persons living within buildings in close proximity to one another." From this perspective, a city would reduce back to the category of substance, since it is understood as a collection of substances. On the other hand, from the standpoint of its form, a city might be defined as "a union of persons, united and governed by law for the sake of bringing about the full perfection of human nature." Here, the genus of the definition is "union," which is a kind of relation. And since a relation is an accident, and therefore incomplete in its being, the proper subject of this relation, "persons," is also included in its definition (see the *Definitions of Complete and Incomplete Things* above on page 37).

Conclusion

This concludes the section on the art of definition. The student should be aware, however, that the discovery and formulation of definitions is not simply a matter of mechanical procedure. Sometimes an important definition is a major work of reason. Moreover, since this is an introductory course, many significant refinements which are essential for discovering more subtle definitions have not been covered.[13] Therefore, the student should not expect that he will be able to define everything using only the tools discussed here. Nevertheless, the tools we have provided should be an aid to the student in this matter.

Exercises

Define the following terms:

chair	bookcase	bicycle
two	seven	octagon

[13] Even if the student had all the tools available to the logician, he would not be able to complete most definitions. Logic approaches definitions based upon the distinctions in the way men *speak* about things, and since only the more obvious distinctions in reality are reflected in speech (for example, the distinction between substance and accident is reflected in the mode in which we signify a substance and an accident in our speech), it follows that logic will typically be able to provide the student with the beginnings of a definition, while some further science will provide him with the distinctions he needs to complete the definition. Thus, for example, the marine biologist will be able to complete the definition of "fish" that the logician starts.

cube	fish	bird
tree	unit	point
silver	virtue	culture
civilization	friendship	beauty
music	marriage	education
religion	happiness	evil

CHAPTER 8

The Art about Statements

A statement is speech which signifies something true or false. A statement is not the only kind of sentence, but it is the only kind of sentence which signifies the true or the false. Compare the following three sentences: Go to the store. I went to the store. Should I go to the store? On the face of it, they may seem very much alike. But one is a statement and the others are not. When a sentence signifies a command or a question, it does not signify that something is or is not so. On the other hand, a statement signifies that something is or is not so.

When a statement signifies that what is, is so (for example, the number three is odd), or when a statement signifies that what is not, is not so (for example, three is not even), then this statement is true. On the other hand, when a statement signifies that what is, is not so (for example, five is not greater than four), or when a statement signifies that what is not, is so (for example, four is greater than five), then this statement is false. So truth and falsity depend upon whether a statement signifies something which agrees with reality.

Truth is the conformance of the mind with reality.

Often, we do not know or cannot even determine whether a given statement is true or false. Nevertheless, we do know that it cannot be both true and false at the same time. It has to be one or the other. In certain cases, a statement is neither true nor false. For example, consider a statement about a future event which is not necessary, like: I will get an A on my next test. Although this statement is not true or false yet, it will at some time be true or false, and so it still falls under the definition of statement given above. So we could give a more refined definition of statement as *speech which signifies something true or false, either actually or potentially.*

The Genera (Kinds) of Statements

Some statements are simple; others are compound. In a simple statement, one thing, and one thing alone, is affirmed or denied of another. For example, "man is an animal" or "man is not a stone." A compound statement is composed of simple statements. Three kinds of compound statements are particularly important in logic: the *and* statement, the *if-then* statement, and the *either-or* statement. An example of the *and* statement is "I ran to the store *and* I bought an ice cream." An example of the *if-then* statement is "*If* a man is a saint, *then* he will go to heaven." An example of the *either-or* statement is "A number is *either* odd *or* even." Notice that the simple and the compound statements are called "statements" equivocally by reason rather than univocally. This is because a statement is speech signifying the true and the false, but true and false mean something different in the simple statement rather than in the compound statements, as we shall see later. Since the compound statement is composed of simple statements, we will examine simple statements first.

The Composing Parts of a Simple Statement

Whenever we want to understand something, it is generally useful to break it down into its parts. This is a universal rule applicable to every branch of knowledge. What are the parts of a statement then? If we treat a statement as an integral whole, then we can divide a simple statement into either two or three parts.

One way to divide a simple statement is to divide it into two parts—namely, a noun and a verb. Both a noun and a verb are kinds of words or names (speech having no parts which signify by themselves), but the noun signifies without any reference to time, while a verb signifies with some reference to time. For example, in the statement *man walks*, *man* is a word which signifies something, but without time. But the word *walks* signifies with time since it indicates something happening in the present. Because a verb signifies with time, it can have several tenses, such as *walked*, signifying the past, or *will walk*, signifying the future. A verb is also a sign of something said of a subject. Thus, a verb always implies some subject (in this example, *walks* is a sign of a particular kind of motion said of *man*). Therefore, we can define a *noun* as *a word which signifies without time*, and we can define a *verb* as *a word which signifies with time, and which is a sign of something said of a subject.*

We can also divide a simple statement into three parts by further dividing the verb into a copula and a predicate. In these cases, the verb is expressed as a combination of the verb "to be" and a predicate; for example, man is walking, or man is animal. In these examples, "man" is the subject, "is" is the copula, and "walking" and "animal" are predicates.

The Species of a Simple Statement

A simple statement can also be treated as a universal whole which can be divided into different kinds or species. If we consider the quality of a statement, then we can divide statement into *affirmative* and *negative* statements. An example of an affirmative statement is "trees are plants." An example of a negative statement is "trees are not plants." Affirmative and negative statements are different species of statements because they are different ways of being a statement.

If we consider not the quality but rather the quantity of a statement, we can divide statement into *universal* and *particular*. This is not exactly a division of simple statements into species but more a quantitative division (like the division between bright red and dull red, which does not result in two different species of color). An example of a universal statement is "All trees are plants." An example of a particular statement is "Some trees are plants." When a statement is indefinite ("Trees are plants") or singular ("This tree is a plant"), it can usually be treated as if it were a particular statement.

Contradictory and Contrary Statements

From what we have said, we can infer that every simple statement has an opposite statement which has the same subject and predicate. For example, the opposite of "Man is rational" is "Man is not rational." This important property of statements will be considered in detail.

If we group the various kinds of statements together under the two divisions of affirmative/negative and universal/particular, it is clear that there are four basic possibilities for the kinds of statements. A statement can be a universal affirmative statement in the form "Every A is B." (Logicians conveniently label universal affirmative statements as "**A**" propositions). A statement can also be a universal negative statement in the form "No A is B" (labeled as "**E**" propositions). A statement can also be a particular affirmative statement in the form "Some A is B" (labeled as "**I**" propositions). Finally, a statement can be a particular negative statement in the form "Some A is not B" (labeled as an "**O**" proposition).

	Universal	**Particular**
Affirmative	"A" Proposition —All A is B.	"I" Proposition —Some A is B.
Negative	"E" Proposition —No A is B.	"O" Proposition —Some A is not B.

We said above that every statement has an opposite statement with the same subject and predicate. In fact, it turns out that every statement can be opposed in *two* ways to statements with the same subject and predicate: namely, a statement can be opposed to another statement as its contrary or as its contradictory. We can conveniently represent this schematically in a square (called the "square of opposition" by logicians). An example of the square of opposition is found in *Figure 3*.

A statement is contradictory to another statement with the same subject and predicate when both statements cannot be true at the same time, nor can both statements be false at the same time. In other words, if one of the statements is true, the other must be false, and if one of the statements is false, the other must be true. For example, the statement "*All men are good*" is contradicted by the statement "*Some men are not good*." If the statement "*All men are good*" is true, then it must be false that "*Some men are not good*." Conversely, if it is false that "*All men are good*," then the statement "*Some men are not good*" must be true.

A statement is contrary to another statement with the same subject and predicate when both statements cannot be true at the same time but can be false at the same time. For example, the statement "*All men are good*" is contrary to the statement "*No men are good*." If it is true that "*All men are good*," then it must be false that "*No men are good*." But if it is false that "*All men are good*," it does not follow that the statement "*No men are good*" is true. The statement "*No men are good*" could be false at the same time that the statement "*All men are good*" is false (namely, in the case when some men are good and some men are not good).

It is important to notice that, strictly speaking, both contradiction and contrariety between statements demands that there be the same subject and predicate. Thus, the statement "*All men are good*" is not, strictly speaking, the contradictory of the statement "*Some men are evil*," nor is it contrary to the statement "*All men are evil*."

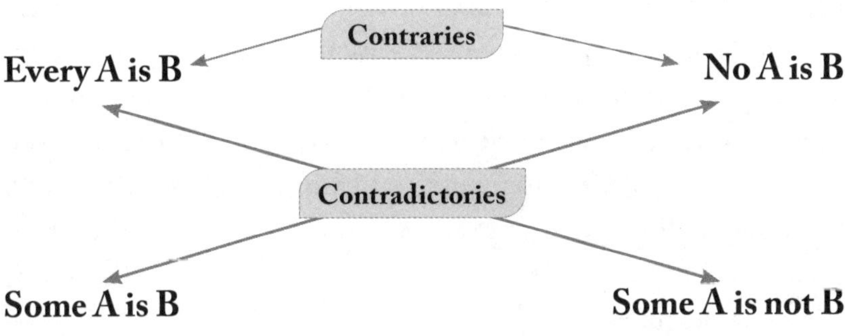

Figure 3

The Composing Parts of a Compound Statement

Each of the compound statements we considered above is composed of two or more simple statements. The *and* statement is composed of simple statements joined by the word "and" between each of the simple statements. An *and* statement may have as many simple statements as you please, so long as there is one fewer *and* than there are simple statements.

The *if-then* statement is composed of two simple statements with an *if* before the first and a *then* before the second. The first statement is called the antecedent, and the second statement is called the consequent. Sometimes an *and* statement can be combined with an *if-then* statement as in the following example: "If I become a priest and I become a religious, then I will be able to offer Mass and wear a religious habit." In this case, the compound statement between the *if* and the *then* is called the antecedent, and the compound statement after the *then* is called the consequent. An *if-then* statement is sometimes called a hypothetical or conditional statement. However, this does not mean that every *if-then* statement is just an hypothesis. Often an *if-then* statement is absolutely certain; for example, "If four is divisible into equal parts, then it is an even number." The *either-or* statement is composed of two or more simple statements with an *either* before the first and an *or* before the others. For example, "Either you are a man or you are not a man." Sometimes, however, we abbreviate these statements by placing the subject first and the *either* before the first predicate and an *or* before the other predicates. For example, "That man is either taller or shorter or the same height as you."

What Do True and False Mean in Compound Statements?

When we say that an *and* statement is true, we mean that all the simple statements of which it is composed are true. But if even one of the simple statements in an *and* statement is false, then the whole *and* statement is false. For example, the statement "Marriage is a sacrament and marriage is only possible between a man and a woman" is true because both of the simple statements composing it are true. But the statement "Marriage is a sacrament and marriage is better than consecrated virginity"[14] is false since the second simple statement is false. On the other hand, when we say that the *if-then* or *either-or* statements are true, we do not mean that the simple statements of which they are composed are true. Take the following example: "If Father Alphonsus is president, then he is the commander in chief of the armed forces." This statement is true, even though the antecedent and the consequent are both false. Take another example: "Either this statement is true or this statement is false." This statement is true, even though one of the simple statements in it is false. What then do we mean when we say that an *if-then* statement is true or false, and what do we mean when we say that an *either-or* statement is true or false? When we say that an *if-then* statement is true, we mean that *the consequent follows from the antecedent necessarily*. And when we say that an *if-then* statement is false, we mean that the consequent does not follow necessarily from the antecedent. For example, the statement "If a man is not a priest, he is not a Catholic" is false because the consequent does not follow necessarily from the antecedent. When we say that an *either-or* statement is true, we mean that *the division given is exhaustive and all-inclusive*. And when we say that an *either-or* statement is false, we mean that the division given is not exhaustive, for there is some other possibility than the ones given. For example, the statement "A man is either a priest or he is married" is false because it is possible for a man to be neither married nor a priest.

In English (as well as many other languages), the meaning of an *either-or* statement can be ambiguous. In this text, whenever we refer to an *either-or* statement, we mean one in which X

14 Cf. Mt 19:12; 1 Cor. 7:7–9; CCC 915–16; Council of Trent, 24th Session, Canon X.

is either A or B, but only one or the other, not both A and B. Sometimes a statement can be taken in a weaker sense, as when I say that a star is either in the universe or in the Milky Way. In this weaker sense, the division is not exclusive, even if it is exhaustive. Finally, an *or* statement can be taken in a still weaker sense, as when I say this man's name is John or this man's name is Bill. In this weakest sense, the statement is true if either of the simple statements composing it are true. We will refer to such statements as *or* statements, but not as *either-or* statements.

Conversion of Simple Statements

Some simple statements can be rearranged so that the subject and the predicate switch places in such a way that the new statement has the same truth as the original statement. This operation is called conversion. An **E** (universal negative) statement can be converted into another **E** statement with the subject and predicates reversed. For example, if no men are trees, then it must also be true that no trees are men. In a similar manner, an **I** (particular affirmative) statement can be converted into another **I** statement with the subject and predicates reversed. For example, if some brown dogs are terriers, then it must also be true that some terriers are brown dogs. An **A** (universal affirmative) statement does not convert completely, but it does convert partially. That is, an **A** statement does not convert into another **A** statement, but rather into an **I** statement. For example, if all dogs are four-legged animals, then some four-legged animals are dogs. The **O** (particular negative) statement does not convert at all.

Conversions
E: No A is B = No B is A.
I: Some A is B = Some B is A.
A: All A is B → Some B is A.
O: Some A is not B → Does not convert.

Statements Which Indicate the Mode of Connection of the Subject and the Predicate

There are many ways in which the subject and predicate of a statement can be connected. Sometimes the subject has to be connected with the predicate as in the statement "the diagonal of a square is incommensurable with its side," but in other cases the subject may or may not be connected with its predicate, as in the statement "A man is sitting," for a man can be sitting or not sitting. When we indicate explicitly in the statement itself the manner, or mode, of connection which the subject has with the predicate, then this kind of a statement is called a *modal statement*. For example, the statement "It is necessary that the sun will rise tomorrow" is a modal statement since the connection between the subject "sun" and the predicate "will rise tomorrow" is expressly stated as being a necessary connection. Again, the statement "It is possible that a man is saved" is a modal statement, since the connection between the subject "man" and the predicate "saved" is expressly stated as being a possible connection.

When comparing the kinds of oppositions which may exist between modal statements, a modal statement which expresses necessity is equivalent to a universal affirmative statement since something which is necessarily connected is connected in every case. On the other hand, a modal statement which expresses possibility or contingency is treated as a particular affirmative statement, since what is possible but not necessary happens in some cases but not all. The oppositions between the various kinds of modal statements is depicted in the figure below.

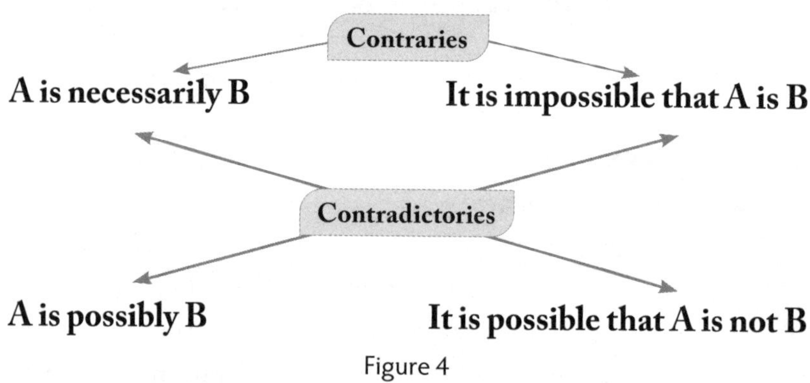

Figure 4

Notice that other synonyms can be inserted to express the same mode of relationship between subject and predicate. For example, instead of the word "possible," the word "contingent" can be used in its place to express the same relationship. Or instead of the word "necessary," the word "must" could be used to the same effect.

Per Se Statements and Self-Evident Statements

Sometimes a statement can only be known to be true with certitude when it is the conclusion of some argument. That is, we have to prove that such a statement is true. But we saw above that not all statements can be this way. For if the truth of all statements had to be proven through an argument, then since the premises of the argument would also have to be proved through another argument (otherwise we wouldn't know if they were true), and this would go on to infinity, it would follow that we could never know whether any statement was true. Therefore, there must be some statements which can be known to be true through themselves without a proof. Such statements are called *self-evident* statements. Some examples of self-evident statements are: the whole is greater than the part; a cause is before its effect; the same thing cannot be and not be at the same time and in the same respect; man is an animal.

Self-evident statements are seen to be true as soon as the meanings of the terms (that is, the words) in the statement are understood. When I say that every bachelor is unmarried, this statement is seen to be true as soon as I understand that the definition of "bachelor" is "an unmarried man." Self-evident statements are distinct from *per se* statements. A *per se* statement need not be self-evident (though many are). What is characteristic of a *per se* statement is that the predicate belongs to the subject on account of what the subject is and not on account of what happens to be connected to the subject. For example, the statements "A triangle is three-sided" and "A triangle has interior angles equal to the sum of two right angles" are both *per se* statements because the predicates "three-sided" and "interior angles equal to the sum of two right angles" belong to the subject "triangle" on account of what a triangle is. But the statement "a triangle is blue" is not *per se*, since the predicate "blue" does not belong to the subject "triangle" on account of what triangle is. Blue is not a way of being triangle, nor does it follow from triangularity. Blue is indifferent to triangles and vice-versa.

To speak more fully, *per se* statements are those whose **necessity** is evident because the predicate belongs to the subject on account of the subject itself (*per* se). Thus, such a statement is *per se*, (a Latin expression meaning "through itself") since the connection of subject and predicate is through the subject itself, without the mediation of some other thing. To put it another way, in a *per se* statement, the subject itself is the cause of the predicate belonging to the subject.

Now all this may sound very difficult, but in practice it is often straightforward to identify a *per se* statement. The easiest way to show that a statement is not *per se* is to identify a case where the subject and the predicate don't go together. Not every triangle is blue, so it is easy to see that "A triangle is blue" is not a *per se* statement. The harder case to see is when the union of subject and predicate don't have any known exceptions. For example, "Every man is in the Milky Way Galaxy" might seem to be a *per se* statement, since there are no known exceptions. But even here, it is easy enough to see that, based upon what man is, there is no inherent reason why man has to exist inside the Milky Way Galaxy. A man must have a body, so a man must be in some place (thus, the statement "Man is somewhere" is a *per se* statement). But there is nothing that prohibits that place from being outside the Milky Way Galaxy. So, with some practice, it can be easy to identify most *per se* statements.

Aristotle distinguished three kinds of *per se* statements:

(1) A statement is *per se* when the predicate is in the definition of the subject. For example, "Every bachelor is unmarried," or "Every man is an animal," or "Every triangle has three sides" are all *per se* in this first sense, since unmarried is in the definition of bachelor, animal is in the definition of man, and three-sided is in the definition of triangle. These kinds of *per se* statements are always self-evident.

(2) A statement is *per se* when the subject is in the definition of the predicate. For example, "Every line is curved or straight," "Every number is odd or even," and "A surface is colored" are all *per se* in this second sense, since line is in the definition of curved and straight, number is in the definition of odd and even, and

surface is in the definition of color (since the proper subject of every color is a surface). When the predicate belongs immediately to the subject, then these kinds of *per se* statements are self-evident. But if the predicate belongs through some middle, as color belongs to a substance through being in a surface, then these statements are not self-evident.

(3) A statement is *per se* when the predicate belongs to the subject as to its proper cause. For example, "The swimming man got wet," "The slaughtered animal died," and "A round thing casts a round shadow." In all these cases, the subject is the proximate cause of the predicate: swimming is the cause of getting wet, slaughtering is the cause of the animal dying, and being round is the cause of casting a round shadow. It is important to see how this third sense of a *per se* statement differs from the previous two senses. In this third sense, the subject is not in the definition of the predicate nor is the predicate in the definition of the subject. Wet is not in the definition of swimming nor is swimming in the definition of wet. Nevertheless, getting wet is a proper effect which is inseparable from the action of swimming. If the predicate belongs to the subject as to its **immediate** proper cause, then such statements are self-evident. Thus, it is self-evident that a swimming man is wet, since there is no intermediate cause between swimming and wet.

It is very important to be aware of these three ways in which a statement can be *per se*, as well as the ways in which a statement is self-evident, since self-evident and *per se* statements are the foundation for all other truths in argumentation. Self-evident and *per se* statements are the anchors which guarantee certitude and necessity to all the other statements which are concluded from them by way of an argument, so they are the most certain and fundamental truths which we can know.

CHAPTER 9

The Art about Syllogism

A syllogism is the most perfect form of argument. There are other forms of argument (such as induction, enthymeme, and example), but all of these others are arguments only to the extent that they resemble a syllogism. A syllogism can be defined as *speech wherein, some premises having been laid down, another statement follows necessarily because of them*. When the premises of a syllogism are simple statements, then the syllogism is called a simple or categorical syllogism. When one premise of a syllogism is an *if-then* statement and the other is a simple statement, then this syllogism is called a hypothetical syllogism. When one premise of a syllogism is an *either-or* statement and the other is a simple statement, then this syllogism is called a disjunctive syllogism. First, we will consider the simple syllogism, and then we will briefly consider the hypothetical and disjunctive syllogisms.

The Form of the Simple Syllogism

As we have already seen, the simple syllogism has two simple statements as premises, and the conclusion which follows from these premises is also a simple statement. The conclusion is not, strictly speaking, a part of the syllogism but rather an effect of the syllogism. Just as a family needs two parents to produce a child, so a syllogism needs two premises to produce a conclusion.

A syllogism does not result by the haphazard throwing together of two statements. The two statements must have a determinate relation to one another before they can come together to form a syllogism. When do two simple statements have the form of a syllogism? *When something else follows necessarily because of the premises.*

Three things are needed here:

1. The conclusion must be different from either premise.

2. The conclusion must follow necessarily from the premises.

3. The conclusion must follow because of the premises.[15]

Let's examine the first requirement: the conclusion must be different from the premises. But how can two statements produce another statement different from either of the premises? The only terms that can be in the conclusion must come from the premises. Therefore, since every statement has a subject and a predicate, the subject and predicate of the conclusion must consist of the terms found in the subjects or predicates of the premises. Obviously, the conclusion cannot take both its subject and predicate from the same premise. For in that case, the conclusion would be the same as one of the premises. So the conclusion must combine two terms found in the premises but without having the same two terms as one of the premises. Therefore, the conclusion must

[15] That is, the conclusion must follow necessarily because of the premises not because of some other thing. For example, given the premises "Figure A has interior angles equal to the sum of two right angles" and "Figure B is the rectilinear figure with the least number of sides," it follows necessarily that figure A is the same as figure B. Nevertheless, that conclusion does not follow necessarily because of those premises but because of some other fact (namely, that both figure A and figure B are triangles).

take one term from one premise and another term from the other premise. So far so good. Taking a term from each premise will ensure that the conclusion is a different statement than either premise. However, it will not ensure that the conclusion follows necessarily or that the conclusion follows because of the premises. Take the following example:

All men are animals.

All trees are living.

All men are living.

It may happen that a true conclusion can be constructed by putting together terms from each premise, but even so, the conclusion does not follow necessarily from the premises, nor is it true because of the premises. How then are we to ensure that the conclusion follows necessarily and is true because of the premises? The only way in which a term in one premise can be necessarily connected to a term in another premise is if each of those terms is necessarily connected to a common or same term. This is vital to understand, as logic cannot proceed without this. It bears repeating: the only way in which a term in one premise can be necessarily connected to a term in another premise is if each of those terms is necessarily connected to a common or same term.

For example:

All men are animals.

All animals are living.

All men are living.

In this argument, both premises have the same term "animal," which is connected to the other terms in both premises. In a syllogism, this same term is called the *middle term*. That is, *the middle term is the term which occurs twice in the premises but is not found in the conclusion*. The middle term is the most important term in a syllogism since it is the linchpin which holds the whole thing together. Logicians also have names for the other two terms in a syllogism: the *major term* and the *minor term*. *The major term is the term which is found in the predicate of the conclusion. The minor term is the term which is found in the subject of the conclusion*. Let's look at the previous syllogism and identify the various parts.

All men are animals.

<u>All animals are living.</u>

All men are living.

Here, "living" is the major term (the term found in the predicate of the conclusion); "men" is the minor term (the term found in the subject of the conclusion); "animals" is the middle term (the term which is connected to the other terms).

Additionally, in a syllogism, "major" and "minor" also apply to the premises. The premise which contains the major term is called the *major premise*. The premise which contains the minor term is called the *minor premise*. In the syllogism above, "All animals are living" is the major premise, "All men are animals" is the minor premise, and "All men are living" is the conclusion. Thus "major" and "minor" are applied both to terms and premises, but primarily to terms.

But why is one term called the major term (as if it were the bigger term) and the other term called the minor term (as if it were the smaller term)? The reason is that a term which is found in the predicate of a statement is always considered to be more universal than the term found in the subject of a statement. That is to say, the major term (the term in the predicate) is always considered to be more universal than the minor term (the term found in the subject). In short, major terms are more universal than minor terms.

Let's take an example with fictional names: All hebits are muckles. We have no idea what a hebit or a muckle is, but we do know that if this statement is true, muckles must be more universal than hebits. For if all hebits are muckles, muckles must cover at least all the hebits, and perhaps something more. If there were more hebits than muckels, this statement could never be true. So the predicate must always be more universal than the subject if a universal statement is to be true.

There is the exception when the predicate and subject are exactly equal in extension, as in the following example: All men are risible. In this case, the statement can be converted to another A statement: All risible beings are men. Statements where the subject and predicate are equal in extension are called *universally commensurate* statements. But even in a universally commensurate statement, the predicate has the note or notion of being more universal, even if it is not so in fact. And for this reason, any term in the predicate of a statement is considered to be more universal than the term which is the subject of that same statement.

So far, we have seen that every syllogism has three terms: a major, middle, and minor term. From the possible positions of the middle term in relation to the other two terms (since the major term is always more universal than the minor term), we can determine that there are three different forms which a syllogism can take. Logicians call the three forms of syllogisms *figures*. In the first figure, the middle term is between the major term and the minor term (that is, it is middle in universality). In the second figure, the middle term is more universal than the major and the minor term (that is, greatest in universality). And in the third figure, the middle term is less universal than the major and the minor term (that is, it is least in universality).

Since these are the only three possibilities, there can only be three figures of syllogism. Since the universality of the middle term is determined by whether it is a subject or a predicate, we can define the three figures as follows: the *first figure* is the figure of syllogism where *the middle term is the subject of one premise and the predicate in the other premise.* The *second figure* is the figure of syllogism where *the middle term is in the predicate of both premises.* And the *third figure* is the figure of syllogism where *the middle term is the subject in both premises.* So the form of each figure can be represented schematically in the following diagrams, where *A* represents the minor term, *B* represents the middle term, and *C* represents the major term. It is typical in logic books to state the major premise first and the minor premise second, so I will follow that convention throughout this chapter:

	B is C
First Figure:	A is B
	C is B
Second Figure:	A is B
	B is C
Third Figure:	B is A

Although we have expressed the premises in the diagrams as affirmative statements (this is that), it should be appreciated that the premises in each figure may also be negative statements, such as "A is not B" or "No A is B."

Up to this point, we have seen that for two premises to come together to form a syllogism, the premises must share a common middle term. We have also seen that there are three possible figures which a syllogism can have. But it still remains to be seen whether a syllogism results whenever two premises which have a common middle term come together. Let us take two examples from the first figure. Remember that:

	B is C
First Figure:	A is B
(I)	All rational animals are risible. All men are rational animals
(II)	No stones are animals. No men are stones.

In these two examples, we see that in the first case (I), a conclusion follows necessarily because of the premises (namely, the conclusion that *all men are risible*), but that in the second case (II), no conclusion follows from the premises. Someone might be tempted to conclude that "all men are animals" from the second case, but while that is a true statement, it does not follow from the premises. Why? This can be clearly seen by replacing the term *animal* with the term *tree*. For then a conclusion with a contrary form would be true: "No men are trees." Similar examples can be taken from the second and third figures as well to show that sometimes a conclusion necessarily follows because of the premises, but at other times no conclusion follows in each of these figures. Evidently, then, it is not enough for two statements to have a common middle term. Something else is required before we can be sure that two statements come together to form a syllogism.[16]

To determine whether or not two statements which share a middle term come together to form a syllogism, we must also consider whether these statements are **A**, **E**, **I**, or **O** statements. That is, we need to consider whether they are affirmative or negative, universal or particular. Since every syllogism requires two premises (the major and the minor), and since there are four kinds of premises (**A**, **E**, **I**, or **O**) possible for both the major and the minor premise, it can easily be seen that there are sixteen (four squared) possible arrangements of statements for each figure of syllogism. Since there are three types of figures of syllogisms, we end up with a total of forty-eight possible forms of syllogisms. Each of these possible arrangements are called the *cases* or *moods* of each figure. The fourteen valid cases—cases that are in the form of a perfect syllogism—are represented in the tables in the appendix. In these tables, as before, I have put the major premise on top and the minor premise on the bottom, since this arrangement is typical in logic texts.

It is possible to demonstrate which cases of each figure are syllogisms and which are not. However, this demonstration is somewhat involved and is better taken up in a more advanced logic class. Nevertheless, an easier method can be used which is just as effective for manifesting which cases of each figure are syllogisms and which are not.

Let us employ this method for the four universal cases of the first figure (that is, the cases of the first figure where both premises are universal). If two premises come together to form a

[16] See the appendix: the sixteen possible cases for each of the three figures of syllogism.

syllogism, then we should never be able to find an example where, if both premises are true, the conclusion is not true. Examine the following two cases:

	Case I:		Case II:
(**A**)	Every B is C.	(**E**)	No B is C.
(**A**)	Every A is B.	(**A**)	Every A is B.
	Every A is C.		No A is C.

Substitute words for A, B, and C in each so that the premises are always true.

For example, in Case I, the case which has two **A** premises, substitute: A=dog, B=mammal, C=animal. With these examples, the conclusion is "Every dog is an animal." In fact, no matter what examples you substitute in for A, B and C, so long as the premises are true, a conclusion in the form every A is C will also be true. And therefore, the case in the first figure where the two premises are **A** statements is a syllogism, since a conclusion which is other than the premises (namely, the conclusion "Every A is C") follows necessarily because of the premises. Let's look at the other case. Remember that:

	Case II:
(**E**)	No B is C.
(**A**)	Every A is B.
	No A is C.

Now, for Case II, the case which has an **A** and an **E** premise, substitute: A=dog, B=mammal, C=stone. With these examples, the conclusion is "No dog is a stone." In fact, no matter what examples you substitute in for A, B, and C, so long as the premises are true, a conclusion in the form *No A is C* will also be true. And therefore, the case in the first figure where the two premises are **A** and **E** statements is a syllogism, since a conclusion which is other than the premises (namely, the conclusion "No A is C") follows necessarily because of the premises.

Therefore, these two cases of the first figure are syllogisms.

But now let us consider the other two universal cases of the first figure.

(I):	(II):
(**A**) Every B is C.	(**E**) No B is C.
(**E**) No A is B.	(**E**) No A is B.

Now substitute words for A, B, and C so that the premises are true.

For example, in (I), the case which has an **E** and an **A** premise, substitute: A=stone, B=dog, C=animal. In this case, both premises are true since no stone is a dog, and every dog is an animal. But how are the major and minor terms related? Well, with these examples, since no stone is an animal, the conclusion would be in the form "No A is C." But what if we substitute different examples: A=cat, B=dog, C=animal. Then the premises are still true since no cat is a dog and every dog is an animal. But in this case, since every cat is an animal, our conclusion takes the form: "Every A is C." So depending upon our examples, we can conclude from these premises both that *No A is C* and that *Every A is C.* That is, we can come to contrary conclusions even when the premises are true. Hence nothing is always so when the premises are true. And this means that there is no perfect syllogism here.

Try to show the same with (II), the case that has the two **E** premises. Substitute the following examples: A=Collie, B=cat, C=cow or dog. Again, it can be seen with these examples that from these two **E** premises, even if they are true, one can conclude either that *No A is C* or that *Every A is C*. Given that there are two **E** premises, it is not necessary to conclude that A and C are related in any definite manner, so no syllogism results. For this reason, both of these cases are labeled as invalid in the first figure table to indicate that these two statements do not come together to form a syllogism.

If this method is followed throughout all the forty-eight possible cases of the three figures, one will discover that there are four cases which are in the form of a syllogism in the first figure, four cases which are in the form of a syllogism for the second figure, and six cases which are in the form of a syllogism in the third figure. Thus, as shown in the tables in the appendix, there are a total of fourteen possible syllogistic forms.

Notice that in the tables some of the cases or moods are labeled as defective rather than invalid. The reason for this is that in these cases a conclusion follows necessarily, but in such a way that the established order of the major and minor terms is not preserved. For example, a term which is in the major premise is placed as the minor term in the conclusion or vice-versa. Since the major term is, by definition, apt to be more universal than the minor term, and since nothing can be apt to be both more and less universal in relation to the same term at the same time, it follows that there is a defective syllogism when the relative universality of the terms is inverted within the same argument.[17] Therefore, we will restrict

---

[17] This question, like the questions about the so-called "fourth figure," require a more advanced treatment than an introductory text can provide, and so I will omit such a treatment here.

ourselves to the fourteen forms from which a conclusion follows perfectly and directly.

Some Tips on How to Determine If We Have Drawn a Correct Conclusion

If we examine the four moods or cases of the first figure, we notice that only those whose major premise is universal and whose minor premise is affirmative form syllogisms. If we examine the second figure, we discover that all the conclusions from syllogisms in the second figure must be negative. Finally, if we examine the third figure, we notice that all the conclusions of the syllogisms in the third figure are particular. The following are some very helpful rules of thumb which can help a beginner to avoid errors:

1. *Nothing follows from two negative statements.*

2. *Nothing follows from two particular statements.*

3. *The middle term must either be the predicate in a negative premise or the subject in a universal premise or both.*

This rule is commonly called the rule of the *distributed middle* by logicians. A term is said to be distributed if it is the subject of a universal premise or the predicate of a negative premise.[18] I call this last rule of thumb the SUNPIN rule, as an acronym for the phrase: **S**ubject in a **UN**inversal premise or the **P**redicate **I**n a **N**egative premise. St. Thomas Aquinas is represented in iconography with a blazing sun pinned on his chest. So just

[18] No need to worry about why the word "distributed" is used to describe this, since this is just a practical rule of thumb. The only thing you need to remember is subject in a universal premise and/or predicate in a negative premise.

remember this SUNPIN and you will be able to remember this rule of thumb.

Using these rules of thumb, you can determine whether or not your syllogism is valid in every case—*except one*. The one case is the **AO** syllogism found in the top right-hand corner of the table for the first figure of syllogisms.[19] In this case, you have a distributed middle (rule 3 is satisfied), you don't have two particular premises (rule 2 is satisfied), and you don't have two negative premises (rule 1 is satisfied). Nevertheless, no conclusion follows in this one case.[20]

Once you have determined if your syllogism is valid, you can use two other rules of thumb to help you figure out what your conclusion should be.

4. *The conclusion must not be stronger than the premises.*

What does this mean? An affirmative statement is stronger than a negative statement, and a universal statement is stronger than a particular statement.[21] Therefore, the strongest statements are those which are universal and affirmative (**A** statements, "All A

[19] All B is C.
Some A is not B.
INVALID

[20] I call this exception the "Harry Belafonte exception." Harry Belafonte was famous for the "Banana Boat Song" with its opening line of "Day-O!" which sounds like AO!

[21] One way to see this order is to consider who knows more: the one who is certain of the truth of a universal statement (every man is mortal) or the one who is only certain of the truth of a particular statement (Julius Caesar is mortal)? And again, who knows more: the one who is sure of an affirmative statement (man has an immortal soul) or the one who is only sure about the truth of a negative statement (man cannot fly)? It clearly requires more knowledge to make universal and affirmative statements.

is B"), and the weakest statements are those which are particular and negative (**O** statements, "Some A is not B").

Strength of statements:

- A > E (universal affirmative is stronger than universal negative)
- A > I (universal is stronger than particular)
- A > O (universal affirmative is stronger than particular negative)
- E > O (universal is stronger than particular)
- I > O (particular affirmative is stronger than particular negative)

Thus, if either premise in a syllogism is negative, then the conclusion must be negative; a syllogism with an **E** or an **O** statement in the premises cannot produce a conclusion with an **A** or **I** statement. And if either premise is particular, then the conclusion must be particular; a syllogism with premises containing either an **I** or an **O** statement cannot produce a conclusion with an **A** or **E** statement. Thus, for example, a syllogism which has a premise which is negative and a premise (either the same one or the other one) which is particular will necessarily have a particular negative (**O**) conclusion. This rule of thumb will help you determine whether your strongest conclusion is an **A**, **E**, **I**, or **O** statement.

5. *A term which is distributed in the conclusion must also be distributed in the premises.*

This rule of thumb helps you to see which term from the premises should be placed in the predicate of the conclusion and which in the subject of the conclusion.

Let's take an example to apply these rules of thumb. Consider the following syllogism:

No B is C.

Some B is A.

Does a conclusion follow necessarily? And if so, what conclusion? Applying rules 1–3, we see that there are not two negative premises (the second premise is affirmative), nor are there two particular premises (the first premise is universal). Moreover, the SUNPIN rule applies, since the middle term "B" is the subject in a universal premise (the first premise). It's in the third figure, so we don't have to worry about the one exception (which is found only in the first figure). So we have a valid syllogism.

What is the strongest conclusion we can draw from these premises? Well, applying rule 4, since one premise is particular and one premise is negative, the strongest conclusion we can get is a particular negative (**O**) conclusion. Finally, applying rule 5, we see that since "C" is distributed in the premises (since it is the **P**redicate **I**n a **N**egative premise), "C" must also be distributed in the conclusion. But since the conclusion is *particular* negative, the only way "C" can be distributed in the conclusion is if it is placed in the predicate. So our conclusion must be "Some A is not C."

Reduction Back to the First Figure[22]

Remember, our different figures for syllogisms:

	B is C
First Figure:	A is B

[22] Supplementary text: Reduction back to the first figure from *Logic: the Art of Defining and Reasoning* by J. Oesterle, chapter 17.

	C is B
Second Figure:	A is B
	B is C
Third Figure:	B is A

Why do we arrange the figures by first, second, and third? What makes one to come before another?

The first figure is called first for a reason: it is first because it is clearer and more powerful. It is clearer to us because it follows our mind's natural way of reasoning about things. It is more powerful because it can conclude even to a universal affirmative statement. It is easy to see that if all A is B, and all B is C, then all A is C. It is not so easy, however, to see that a conclusion follows in the second and third figures. So the first figure is the perfect form of syllogism, while the second and third figures are less perfect. And since something less perfect is only able to be understood completely in light of that which is perfect, it follows that the only way to really understand the second and third figures is to see them in light of the first figure. Aristotle was the first to show that all the syllogistic forms of the second and third figures can be shown to be syllogisms by means of the first figure. Although this can be done for all ten syllogisms of the second and third figures, we will take only one simple case from the second figure. In the second figure, the following argument is a syllogism:

No C is B.

All A is B.

No A is C.

We can now use the first figure to show that this same conclusion follows from these premises. First, take the top premise: "No C is B." Now, using our rules for converting statements, we notice that we can convert "No C is B" to "No B is C." We can now put the converted statement together with the other original premise to get the following first figure syllogism:

No B is C.

<u>All A is B.</u>

No A is C.

Thus, if we were not sure whether or not the conclusion "No A is C" followed from the premises "All A is B" and "No C is B," we could use the first figure, which is clearer to us, to manifest that this conclusion does follow. A similar method can be used for the other syllogisms in the second and third figures to render them into first figure arguments.

The Form of the If-Then Syllogism

Recall that the if-then syllogism consists of an if-then statement followed by a simple statement. There are only four possible forms which this kind of an argument can take:

1. If A then B
<u>A is so</u>

2. If A then B
<u>B is so</u>

3. If A then B
<u>A is not so</u>

4. If A then B
<u>B is not so</u>

Notice that here the letters *A* and *B* stand for simple *statements*, not for *words*. Let's apply what we've learned: Examine each of these four forms to determine whether or not, given that the premises are true, anything follows necessarily because of the premises applying the rules from this chapter.

If you analyzed these four forms correctly, you discovered that the first and the last forms were syllogisms but that the middle two are not syllogisms. Let us manifest this through examples. (1) If this priest is a religious, then he has taken vows; this priest is a religious. Therefore, it follows that he has taken vows. Thus, the conclusion of the first form is "*B is so.*" (2) If this priest is a religious, then he has taken vows; this priest has taken vows. But does it follow that he is a religious? No. Perhaps he took some vows other than religious vows. (3) If this animal is pregnant, it is a female; this animal is not pregnant. Does it follow that it is not a female? No. An animal can be female without being pregnant. (4) If this animal is pregnant, it is a female; this animal is not a female. Therefore, this animal is not pregnant. For if not, then this animal is pregnant. But if this animal were pregnant, it would follow from the first form of the if-then syllogism that this animal is a female, which is contradictory to one of the premises we already assumed to be true. Therefore, the conclusion of the fourth form is "*A is not so.*"

Earlier we saw that the truth of the if-then statement does not depend upon the truth of its simple statements but rather upon the necessary connection between the two simple statements in the if-then statement. Because of this, it is possible to arrive at a true conclusion with necessity from an if-then syllogism *even if the antecedent of the if-then statement is false.* A famous example of this is Aristotle's argument in Book VI of his *Physics* that every mobile is in motion through something else. At one point in the argument, he uses the following if-then syllogism:

> If something having parts were not in motion in virtue of its parts being in motion, then stopping the part would not stop the whole.
>
> But stopping the part does stop the whole.
>
> Therefore, whatever has parts is moved in virtue of those parts being in motion.

This syllogism is of the form "If A then B, B is not so, therefore A is not so." Notice that the antecedent of the if-then statement is false. Nevertheless, the conclusion is true and follows necessarily.

The Form of the Either-Or Syllogism

Recall that the either-or syllogism consists of an either-or statement followed by one or more simple statements. The following are either-or syllogisms:

X is either A or B.	X is either A or B or C.
X is not A.	X is not A.
Therefore, X is B.	X is not B.
	Therefore, X is C.

Notice that the number of simple statements after the either-or statement is one less than the number of possible cases, since all but one of the possibilities must be ruled out in order to arrive at a necessary conclusion.

We can also argue in another way using the either-or syllogism. Consider the following case:

Y is either A or B.

X is not A.

X is not B.

Therefore, X is not Y.

If we argue in this form, the number of simple statements after the either-or statement must be equal to the number of possible cases, since all the possibilities must be ruled out in order to arrive at a necessary conclusion. Remember that for an either-or statement to be true, the division given must be exhaustive (that is, it must cover all the possibilities).

If the division given in the either-or statement is not only exhaustive but also exclusive (so that A is never B and vice-versa), then other forms of argument using the either-or syllogism are as follows:

X is either A or B (but not both).

X is not A.

Therefore, X is B.

X is either A or B (but not both).

X is A.

Therefore, X is not B.

Exercises

Determine whether any of the following are syllogisms. Indicate the middle term, if there is one, and determine the figure. Finally, if a conclusion follows necessarily from the premises, state what conclusion follows and identify the major and minor terms.

All herbivores are vegetarians.
All cows are herbivores.

Some mortals are rational.
All men are mortal.

All B is C.
Some A is B.

Some man is not tall.
No short person is tall.

Some students are diligent.
No sloth is diligent.

All teachers are good.
All teachers are fair.

Some planes are fast.
No jet is slow.

No machines are animals.
All cars are machines.

All invisibles are transparent.
No color is invisible.

No female is male.
All pregnant things are female.

No monkey is a person.
All Americans are humans.

Some C is not B.
All A is B.

All students hate universals.
Some student is not alert.

Some A is not C.
No A is B.

If-Then and Either-Or Syllogisms

If there is an oak tree, then there must have been an acorn.
There is an acorn.

If men are circles, then they have equal radii.
Men do not have equal radii.

Either a surface is colored or transparent.
This surface is not colored.

CHAPTER 10

The Art of Demonstration[23]

Everything we have done so far has been in preparation for what we are about to consider next: the art of demonstration. We said before that some truths are self-evident; that is, they do not need to be proved or demonstrated through other statements known to be true. But the number of these self-evident truths is not great and, although these truths are very certain to us, most of these truths are vague and general, not clear and distinct. Moreover, due to the inherent weakness of the mind of man, who among all spiritual creatures has the weakest knowing power, nearly all the self-evident truths we can know concern things very close to our senses: things which are not very noble in themselves. Therefore, if we are ever to get anywhere really important with our minds, if we are ever to know the truths which are most noble and most perfective of our reason, we need to move from these self-evident truths to truths which are known through arguments and proofs.

Some arguments do not result in conclusions which are very certain or clear. We call such arguments probable or persuasive arguments: arguments where there is some doubt or fear of error that the conclusion might be wrong. And although we should not

[23] Supplementary text: Aristotle, *Posterior Analytics*, Bk. I, ch.1-4.

despise such arguments (since probable knowledge is often the only or best kind of knowledge we can have of some things), we should always seek to obtain the best kind of knowledge possible about a given subject. The best kinds of arguments are called proofs, or *demonstrations*. *A demonstration is a syllogism which causes someone to know a conclusion completely (that is, perfectly)*. These arguments are better than probable arguments for three reasons:

1. They can cause someone to know a conclusion with certitude—that is, without fear of error.

2. They are about things which are necessary—that is, things which are always so.

3. They cause someone to know a conclusion clearly, not in just a confused and general way.

In short, the particular kind of syllogism called the demonstration is the most powerful tool of reason. This is why the art of demonstration is at the pinnacle of logic. All the other parts of logic are in some way ordered to constructing demonstrations.

The Greeks called the knowledge which is concluded from a demonstration *episteme*, which often gets translated as "scientific knowledge." But because of the ambiguity of the term scientific in modern parlance, we will use the expression *reasoned-out knowledge* to indicate knowledge which is the conclusion of a demonstration.

What Is a Demonstration and How Do We Make One?

The above definition of demonstration, *a syllogism causing someone to know a conclusion completely*, is a definition from final cause. Recall that there are four causes (material, formal, agent, and final), and any one of them might be found in an essential definition. Remember also that it is often possible to reason from the final cause of a thing to its material and formal causes. For example, if the final cause of a house is known (to provide shelter from the elements and a comfortable place to live), then we can reason to the fact that it must have a roof and walls to support the roof and foundations to support the walls. And from this we can determine that the materials for the roof, walls, and foundation must be solid and durable materials like wood, stone, or brick. Or to take another example, if someone wants to build a beautiful basilica, like St. Peter's in Rome, he will choose the appropriate materials to make it strong and durable as well as beautiful and well proportioned.

Now, every art is ordered to making or doing, and the art of demonstration is no exception. In fact, a demonstration is very much like a house or a church: it's something that you make from raw materials. So a logician is like an architect, and a demonstration is like the most perfect building he can design and make; demonstrations are like the basilicas of logic. And since we have the final cause of a demonstration, we can reason from it to its material cause. But what are the materials from which a demonstration is made? The premises of course. From our definition of demonstration, therefore, we can reason to the kinds of premises we need to build a demonstration.

Since a demonstration causes someone to know a conclusion completely, its premises must have certain qualities which make them suitable to cause someone to know a conclusion completely. In the second chapter of the first book of his *Posterior Analytics*, Aristotle identified six qualities which every premise of a demonstration must have: The premises of a demonstration must be (1) *true*, (2) *unmiddled*, and (3) *first*. Furthermore, in relation to the conclusion, the premises must be (4) *prior* to the conclusion, (5) *causes* of the conclusion, and (6) *better known* than the conclusion.

Let us now see how these properties of the premises of a demonstration follow from our definition of demonstration. The premises must be *true*, otherwise, they could not cause us to know anything, since false premises cannot cause us to know a true conclusion. The premises must be *unmiddled* (that is, not proved through some middle term in another argument) and *first*, otherwise the conclusion would not be known completely, since the foundational, self-evident truths upon which the conclusion rests would not be known. The premises must be *better known* than the conclusion, otherwise we wouldn't know the conclusion by knowing the premises and the premises would be useless for coming to know the conclusion. Finally, the premises must be *causes* of and *prior* to the conclusion, otherwise we could not know the conclusion completely. The reason for this is that a cause contains the whole of its effect, but an effect does not contain the whole of its cause. Therefore, if we are to know a conclusion entirely or completely, we must know it as an effect of premises which are its causes, not vice-versa. Just as the architect of a basilica will select not just any materials but only the most beautiful marble and strongest stone, the purest gold, etc., so also the logician will select only those premises which have the above-mentioned qualities. Premises which do not meet these qualifications could not go into a syllogism which produces perfect knowledge. Anything less would be unworthy of a demonstration.

But how are we to find premises meeting all of these qualifications? And how will we know that we have them when we find them? Fortunately, we have already seen instances of such statements. Self-evident statements in which the predicate belongs to the subject *per se* (in any of the three senses of *per se* statements) will satisfy the conditions mentioned above. Self-evident and *per se* statements are derived from a process called *induction*, which we shall consider at the end of this chapter.

The Different Kinds of Demonstration

The term "demonstration" is applied to three kinds of arguments. In the strict sense of the word, a syllogism which concludes to a statement from its *proximate and proper cause* is called a demonstration. Thus, in this first case, we reason from cause to effect. In a looser sense, a syllogism which concludes to a statement from its *remote cause* is called a demonstration. This kind of demonstration also proceeds from cause to effect. Finally, in the loosest sense of the word, a syllogism which concludes to a statement from its *effect* is called a demonstration. This kind of demonstration proceeds from effect to cause. Logicians often borrow the Latin expressions for the above types of demonstration and call the first type of demonstration *propter quid* ("on account of what"), and the second and third types *quia* ("that [it is so]").

Let us give examples of each kind of demonstration. The following are demonstrations from proximate and proper cause:

Two is a number measured twice by the unit.

A number measured twice by the unit is an even prime number.

Therefore, two is an even prime number.

Man is rational animal.

A rational animal is grammatical.

Therefore, man is grammatical.

In these two examples, we conclude that a property (even prime number, grammatical) is necessarily connected with a subject (two, man) through its proper cause. The reason why two is an even prime number is because it is measured twice by a unit. For a prime number is a number which is measured only by itself and the unit, while an even number is a number which is divisible into equal parts. Again, the reason why man is grammatical is that he is rational. For an animal is rational if it is capable of seeing order as such, while an animal is grammatical if it is capable of putting order into speech. Therefore, here the premises tell us exactly why (*propter quid*) the conclusion is so.

The following are examples of demonstrations which proceed from remote causes:

A stone is not an animal.

Only animals can breathe.

Therefore, a stone cannot breathe.

A circle is not a polygon.

Only polygons can have three straight sides.

Therefore, a circle does not have three straight sides.

In both of these examples, we are proceeding from cause to effect. But notice that the cause given is not the proper or proximate cause but only something remotely related to the proper cause. For not all animals breathe but only those which have blood and lungs. And not all polygons have three straight sides but only triangles. If we were to give the argument in terms of the proper cause, we would say, for example, "A circle is not a triangle; only triangles have three straight sides; therefore, a circle does not have three straight sides." Or if we wished to keep the same middle term, we could argue, "A circle is not a polygon; only a polygon has straight sides; and therefore a circle does not have straight sides." Nevertheless, we should appreciate that these demonstrations result in certain knowledge, even if they don't tell us *exactly* why the conclusion is true. Thus, we can say that we know that (*quia*) a conclusion is so without knowing exactly why (*propter quid*) it is so.

The following are examples of demonstrations which proceed from effect to cause:

Man is an animal capable of speaking.

Animals which can speak are rational.

Therefore, man is a rational animal.

When the earth casts a shadow on the moon, it is circular.

Whatever casts a circular shadow is round.

Therefore, the earth is round.

In each of these demonstrations the conclusion is actually the cause of the truth signified by one of the premises. For the fact that the man is rational is the reason why he is capable of speech, and the fact that the earth is round is the reason why it causes a circular shadow. But since the effect is better known *to us*, the effect is the *cause of our knowledge of the conclusion*. In this case then, we come to know that (*quia*) the conclusion is so without knowing why it is so (at least with regard to the "why" in things).

There is another way in which an argument can be a demonstration besides the three mentioned above. This occurs in cases where one premise is from one branch of knowledge and the conclusion is in a different branch of knowledge. For example, a doctor may know that circular wounds heal the slowest, but the mathematician knows the reason for this. Here is the demonstration:

A wound heals at a speed proportional to the ratio of the perimeter of the wound to its area.

A circle has the least ratio of perimeter to area.

Therefore, a circular wound heals slowest (i.e., at the least speed).

Since a wound heals by the production of new tissue from the healthy tissue surrounding the wounded area, the wound heals at a rate proportional to the perimeter of the wound (i.e., where there is healthy tissue). This is known by a doctor. But the mathematician knows the second premise—namely, that a circle is the figure with the greatest ratio of area to perimeter. In this case, one premise is from the science of mathematics and the conclusion is from natural philosophy. This means that the term circle means a mathematical circle in the premise but a physical circle in the conclusion. So the cause given is not exactly the proper cause since the cause is applied to abstract circles not physical ones. Nevertheless, it is very much like the proper cause. This case brings up the interesting case of so-called analogous middle terms. We will consider these kinds of middle terms briefly after we consider the different grades of certitude.

Comparing the Different Grades of Certitude

In each of the above arguments, the conclusion is known with certitude. Although two truths can both be held without fear of error—that is, with complete certitude—nevertheless, some of these are more certain than others. For example, if a syllogism has two self-evident premises and a conclusion follows necessarily from them, then both the premises and the conclusion are certain, yet since the conclusion depends upon the premises, the premises are by that very fact more certain. In fact, we can distinguish many different grades or degrees of certitude. If we begin with statements which are least certain to us and move to those which are most certain to us, the order is as follows: in the area of opinion (in which there is some fear of error) there are *belief*, *the conclusions of probable arguments*, and *the premises of probable arguments*. In the area of knowledge (in which there is no fear of error), there are *the conclusions of effect to cause demonstrations*, *the conclusion of cause to effect demonstrations*, *self-evident principles*, and, finally, that which is most certain *supernatural faith*. Supernatural faith is based upon the authority of God, Who is the First Truth and, hence, the foundation of all other truths. Therefore, anything revealed by God is by that very fact more certain than anything else.

Names Which Are Equivocal by Reason

Above, in the chapter about definition, we saw that some names are univocal, while others are equivocal. Univocal names are those which are applied to many things with the same name and the same meaning. For example, animal as said of dog and animal as said of cat has the same meaning, so it is univocal. On the other hand, when the same name is said of many things with a different meaning, then this name is said to be equivocal. So dry as said of wine and dry as said of pavement is equivocal, and bat as said of wooden club and bat as said of flying rodent is equivocal.

Equivocal names can be divided into two groups. If the equivocal names have no order or relation between them—that is, if the same name was just imposed on two things by chance—then these names are called *equivocal by chance*, or purely equivocal. But if there is an order among the meanings of equivocal names—that is, if the same name is imposed upon two things for a reason—then such names are called *equivocal by reason*; some names which are equivocal by reason are called *analogous* names.

Let us examine the following uses of the word "see." I see that tree over there. I can still see my mom the way she used to be when she was young. I see that this statement is true. In these three statements, the word "see" is used in three different, but related, meanings. The first see refers to the sense of sight. The second see refers to an activity within the memory or imagination. The third see refers to an activity in the understanding by way of concepts. These words have different but obviously related meanings. Another example which is perhaps harder to see is the word "demonstration." Demonstration is an analogous term as applied to a *propter quid* syllogism and a *quia* syllogism.

Words which are equivocal by reason are important for philosophy. First of all, since they are closer than words which are equivocal by chance, they are more likely to cause an error, as in the following argument: God is love; love is an emotion; therefore, God is an emotion. If we know how to distinguish such words, we will be more able to avoid mixing up two words with different but related meanings. On the other hand, in some sciences like sacred theology, metaphysics, and natural philosophy, we need to have recourse to words which are equivocal by reason in order to gain knowledge about the subject matter of those sciences. In this way, knowing about words which are equivocal by reason is helpful for philosophy in a positive sense.

Names used equivocally by reason can originate in three ways: (1) those in which a part takes the same name as the whole, such as when we say that dogs are divided into dogs and puppies, or finger is divided into finger and thumb (sometimes we say we have five fingers, and at other times that we have four fingers and a thumb: notice that the more general name of finger does not have the exact same meaning as the more particular name finger, since one includes thumb and the other excludes or is opposed to thumb); (2) those in which the same name is extended to cover something like it because of a proportion, such as when we call the act of understanding "seeing," since understanding is to the intellect as seeing is to the eye; (3) those in which the same name is extended to cover something like it because of one dropping off part of its definition, such as when we call that which makes colors manifest light and that which makes anything manifest light.

Note that these are three ways in which a name comes to be used equivocally by reason. They are not three kinds or species of names used equivocally by reason. In principle, it is possible for the same name to come to be used equivocally by reason in more than one of these three ways. For example, the name light may come to be used equivocally by reason because part of its definition is dropped off (the third way) and also because the mind sees a proportion between sensible light and intelligible light (the second way).

Induction

At the very beginning of our consideration of logic, we encountered the difficulty that whenever we learn something, our knowledge seems to come from pre-existent knowledge. But we cannot have an infinite regress, otherwise we will know nothing at all. So we discovered that there are some premises which are known through themselves, without the aid of a demonstration. We must now consider how we acquire these first, self-evident statements. The process which begets the knowledge of these first premises is called induction.

Induction is an argument which leads from many particulars to a universal. For example, I see a house, which is a whole, and bricks, which are its parts, and I notice that the whole house is bigger than any part of it; I see a tree, which is a whole, and a trunk and branches, which are its parts, and I notice that the whole tree is bigger than any of its parts; I see a pie, which is a whole, and slices, which are its parts, and I notice that the whole pie is bigger than any of its parts. Eventually, I come to a universal statement: every whole is greater than its parts. I have moved from a number of particular statements about particular wholes and parts (houses, pies, etc.) to a universal statement which is simply about the relationship between a whole and part of any kind. Take another example: we see a Great Dane that is large, with short brown hair, has four legs, a tail, and barks; a Collie is medium sized, has long brown and white hair, has four legs, a tail, and barks; a Chihuahua is small, has short black hair, has four legs, a tail, and barks. My mind then attends to what is common and disregards what is peculiar to each to arrive at the conclusion that a dog is an animal with four legs and a tail and which barks. In every case where an induction leads to a universal statement, the universal statement arises from a consideration of what is common to a number of experiences which the induction brings together and orders.

At this point, it will be helpful if each student in class comes up with his own example of an induction. Go around the room to each student and ask him to give an example of an induction. Start with a number of particulars that have something in common, and then see what universal conclusion you can make about all of the particulars together.

A question arises here: Can induction ever lead to certitude? If induction is simply an enumeration of particulars, then unless I have gone through all the particulars, how can I be sure that my universal statement is true? For example, if I have not seen all dogs in the universe, how can I be sure that all dogs bark?

To answer this question, we must distinguish two kinds of induction. There is one kind of induction which does not lead to anything but probable knowledge. For example, I notice that all the squirrels that I see are brown and that all the crows I see are black. After a while, I might come to the conclusion that all squirrels are brown or all crows are black, but this is only probable (in fact there are such things as black and grey squirrels, as well as grey crows). Inductions like this happen all the time in experimental sciences, such as when a physicist notices that no physical body travels faster than light in a vacuum, or that the gravitational mass of every body is equal to its inertial mass. These inductions are sometimes based upon millions of instances, yet they are not absolutely certain. There is nothing that prevents us from supposing it's possible that one day we might find something which travels faster than light, or that there might be a body whose inertial and gravitational mass are unequal. We simply can't be sure in such cases since we don't apprehend the very natures of the things involved in the induction.

But there is another kind of induction which leads up to and terminates in certitude. Examples of such inductions are that the whole is greater than the part, or that every triangle has three sides. If someone comes up and says to you, "Look, here's a triangle with four sides!" you would not think to yourself, "I guess some triangles can have four sides." Instead, you would say to the person, "You just don't understand what the name triangle means; what you are showing me is a quadrilateral, not a triangle!" It is a completely different case than the black squirrel or the grey crow or the dog that doesn't bark. You see right away that having three sides is part of the very "what it is" of a triangle. Something similar would happen if someone tried to show you a dog that wasn't an animal, or a crow that wasn't a bird. You would simply say, "You don't know what the name 'dog' means if you think this thing is a dog even though it's not an animal!"

The reason why we have certitude in the latter cases is that such inductions terminate in an intuition, a direct seeing, of the *very natures* of the things we are considering. After we have considered enough examples, we know what it is to be a whole and a part, and what it is to be a triangle, etc. Thus, in these cases, we can have certain knowledge about the universals acquired through the induction. Our certitude does not come from the fact that the list of examples is exhaustive and complete. Instead, the certitude comes from the human mind's natural ability to know what things are. So the list of examples used in the induction is the cause of someone *coming to know* some universal, even though it is not the cause of them *knowing* that universal. Here's a simple example to explain what I mean. Go outside and find a small object in the distance (e.g., a house on the hillside). Now try to show someone else which object you are looking at by leading him from more obvious landmarks until the other person can see the small object for himself. Notice that once the other person has seen the object for himself, he no longer needs to follow the landmarks that you used to bring his attention to that object. He can see it for himself because he has a natural ability to see it. All he has to do is to direct his eyes to that same place again. In this example, leading someone else by way of obvious landmarks is like induction, while seeing the object for oneself is like the intuition of the universal. The landmarks were needed to *come to see* the object the first time but were not necessary to *see* the object itself. Similarly, induction is needed to *come to know* a universal but is not needed to *know* the universal once the mind has seen it on its own.

Perhaps another sensible analogy to induction will be helpful. Go up to the board with a fairly simple image in mind (for example, a dog or a horse or even a hexagon). Then begin to carefully place points on the board so that these points fall on the imaginary outline of your figure. When enough points are in place, the outline of the figure should become evident to everyone (by simply connecting the dots in their imaginations). Each student should quietly raise his hand when he has become certain of what figure is being represented. Once most or all of the students have raised their hands, the teacher can ask one what figure he is drawing. Notice that the first dot did not cause someone to know what figure was being drawn, nor the second, nor the third. In fact, no individual dot was what caused the students to see the outline. Rather, at some moment in time, each student perceived the *order* among all the dots. This is something qualitatively different than perceiving each of the dots in themselves. Some new power or ability of perception was necessary to perceive the whole figure, above and beyond each of the dots. Something similar happens for induction. The individuals, like each dot, are perceived by the senses, but the universal which is the order among the individuals is perceived by a different power of the soul (the intellect).

In this case, we see that the induction is really a preparation for an act of the mind which is distinct from the process of the induction itself. When a man wants to build a fire, he has to gather wood together and then set it up in the right order so that it will easily catch fire. Only then does he apply the match to the wood. In a similar manner, induction is a gathering and ordering of the materials needed to grasp a universal, but the actual grasping of the universal comes about by the application of the light of the mind to the materials gathered by the induction. This application of the light of the mind to many similar experiences (by which application the universal is acquired) is sometimes called *intuition*. The induction takes time, but the intuition happens all at once. So induction is like a process or a road which leads up to an intuition, which is like the destination at the end of the road. First, there is the induction over time, and then something qualitatively different happens all at once, and a universal is formed through an act of the mind.

This ends our consideration of logic for the quarter. Logic, like many other disciplines, is not acquired perfectly in a short time. Nevertheless, it is helpful to make a good beginning. The student is encouraged to continue to perfect his reasoning skills through advanced studies in logic.

Exercises

1. Are the following names *univocal*, *equivocal by chance*, or *equivocal by reason*?

A. *Fan* said of sports spectator and a machine with spinning blades.

B. *Crane* said of a bird and a device used for construction.

C. *Dry* said of a cloth and a sponge.

D. *Dry* said of wine and a sponge.

E. *Dry* said of humor and wine.

F. *Many* as opposed to one and many as opposed to few.

G. *Form* said of a triangle and a syllogism.

H. *Love* said of an emotion and an act of the will.

I. *False* said of a statement and gold.

J. *Good* said of what pleases the senses and what is reasonable.

K. *Beautiful* said of a picture and an idea.

L. *Thing* said of a man and a horse.

M. *Thing* said of a man and his health.

N. *Animal* said of a man and a horse.

O. *Part* said of a brick in a house and a species in a genus.

P. *In* as when a part is in a whole and when a conclusion is in its premises.

2. Determine if the following arguments are demonstrations *propter quid* or *quia*.

A. Two is a number measured twice by the unit.
A number measured twice by the unit is the first prime number.
Two is the first prime number.

B. Man is a rational animal.
A rational animal is capable of perceiving order as order.
Man is capable of perceiving order as order.

C. Man is a grammatical animal.
A grammatical animal is rational.
Man is a rational animal.

D. Every mobile has a material principle.
Whatever has a material principle is divisible.
Every mobile is divisible.

E. The human will is not determined to some particular act.
Whatever is not determined to a particular act is immaterial.
The human will is immaterial.

F. The human intellect is immaterial.
That which is immaterial can grasp the universal as such.
The human intellect can grasp the universal as such.

G. An angel is not a living body.
Only living bodies produce offspring.
Angels do not have offspring.

H. An angel is not a living body.
Whatever is not a living body does not have sensation.
An angel does not have sensation.

First Figure

All B is C **All A is B** **All A is C** **VALID**	All B is C No A is B *Some C is not A* **DEFECTIVE**	**All B is C** **Some A is B** **Some A is C** **VALID**	All B is C Some A is not B **INVALID**
No B is C **All A is B** **No A is C** **VALID**	No B is C No A is B **INVALID**	**No B is C** **Some A is B** **Some A is not C** **VALID**	No B is C Some A is not B **INVALID**
Some B is C All A is B **INVALID**	Some B is C No A is B *Some C is not A* **DEFECTIVE**	Some B is C Some A is B **INVALID**	Some B is C Some A is not B **INVALID**
Some B is not C All A is B INVALID	Some B is not C No A is B **INVALID**	Some B is not C Some A is B **INVALID**	Some B is not C Some A is not B **INVALID**

Second Figure

All C is B All A is B **INVALID**	**All C is B** **No A is B** **No A is C** **VALID**	All C is B Some A is B **INVALID**	**All C is B** **Some A is not B** **Some A is not C** **VALID**
No C is B **All A is B** **No A is C** **VALID**	No C is B No A is B **INVALID**	**No C is B** **Some A is B** **Some A is not C** **VALID**	No C is B Some A is not B **INVALID**
Some C is B All A is B **INVALID**	Some C is B No A is B *Some C is not A* **DEFECTIVE**	Some C is B Some A is B **INVALID**	Some C is B Some A is not B **INVALID**
Some C is not B All A is B *Some C is not A* **DEFECTIVE**	Some C is not B No A is B **INVALID**	Some C is not B Some A is B **INVALID**	Some C is not B Some A is not B **INVALID**

Third Figure

<table>
<tr><td>All B is C
<u>All B is A</u>
Some A is C
VALID</td><td>All B is C
<u>No B is A</u>
Some C is not A
DEFECTIVE</td><td>All B is C
<u>Some B is A</u>
Some A is C
VALID</td><td>All B is C
<u>Some B is not A</u>
Some C is not A
DEFECTIVE</td></tr>
<tr><td>No B is C
<u>All B is A</u>
Some A is not C
VALID</td><td>No B is C
<u>No B is A</u>
INVALID</td><td>No B is C
<u>Some B is A</u>
Some A is not C
VALID</td><td>No B is C
<u>Some B is not A</u>
INVALID</td></tr>
<tr><td>Some B is C
<u>All B is A</u>
Some A is C
VALID</td><td>Some B is C
<u>No B is A</u>
Some C is not A
DEFECTIVE</td><td>Some B is C
<u>Some B is A</u>
INVALID</td><td>Some B is C
<u>Some B is not A</u>
INVALID</td></tr>
<tr><td>Some B is not C
<u>All B is A</u>
Some A is not C
VALID</td><td>Some
B is not C
<u>No B is A</u>
INVALID</td><td>Some B is not C
<u>Some B is A</u>
INVALID</td><td>Some B is not C
<u>Some B is not A</u>
INVALID</td></tr>
</table>